DEPRESSION

We would like to dedicate this book to our husbands, Eric Toner and
Howard Freeland, and our children, Kaitlin Toner Raimi, Kendra Barrett,
Rhianna Toner, Rachel Freeland, and David Freeland.—*JBT & CABF*

Published by
MAGINATION PRESS®
An Educational Publishing Foundation Book
American Psychological Association
750 First Street, NE
Washington, DC 20002

Magination Press is a registered trademark of the American Psychological
Association.

For more information about our books, including a complete catalog,
please write to us, call 1-800-374-2721, or visit our website at
www.apa.org/pubs/magination.

Composition by Circle Graphics, Columbia, MD
Cover and design by Laura Huliska Beith
Printed by Lake Book Manufacturing, Inc., Melrose Park, IL

Library of Congress Cataloging-in-Publication Data
Names: Toner, Jacqueline B., author. | Freeland, Claire A. B., author.
Title: Depression : a teen's guide to survive and thrive / by Jacqueline B.
  Toner, PhD and Claire A.B. Freeland, PhD.
Description: Washington, DC : Magination Press, [2016]
Identifiers: LCCN 2016012845 (print) | LCCN 2016014859 (ebook) | ISBN
  9781433822742 (pbk.) | ISBN 1433822741 (pbk.) | ISBN 9781433822759 () |
  ISBN 143382275X ()
Subjects: LCSH: Depression in adolescence—Treatment. | Cognitive therapy.
Classification: LCC RJ506.D4 T66 2016 (print) | LCC RJ506.D4 (ebook) | DDC
  616.85/2700835—dc23
LC record available at https://lccn.loc.gov/2016012845

Manufactured in the United States of America

10 9 8 7 6 5 4 3 2 1

DEPRESSION

A TEEN'S GUIDE TO

SURVIVE

AND

THRIVE

BY
JACQUELINE B. TONER, PHD
AND
CLAIRE A.B. FREELAND, PHD

Magination Press • American Psychological Association • Washington, DC

CONTENTS

Contents

A NOTE TO YOU, OUR READER

As a teen you get a great deal of information and guidance on lots of things. If you take a course on study skills, your teacher will no doubt make lots of suggestions about how to approach projects or memorize information. If you are about to take a standardized test for college admissions, you will probably get advice about how to interpret tricky questions or whether to guess on answers. The list goes on, right?

But you may get no direct instruction about how to manage difficult emotions. It may seem that you're expected to just know how to cope with all the changes and challenges you're facing. This lack of direction can be hard because you are at an age when you are vulnerable to depression. While people often use the word "depression" to describe a momentary mood, the same term is also used to label a more serious and long-lasting problem that can interfere with many aspects of your life. It's that second definition we'll be focusing on in this book.

If you're like most kids your age, you may have heard of depression, and you may even have some idea of what it is. But if you are experiencing depression, you definitely need to understand it better. More important, you'll want to learn effective ways to interrupt depression, cope with it, or avoid it altogether. We think you deserve a book just for you to explain what depression is, how it may derail you, and effective ways to prevent depression or to take care of yourself if you are depressed.

IS THIS BOOK FOR YOU?

You may have picked up this book because of difficulties you are experiencing or upsetting emotions you have. Or you may just be curious about what you've heard or read about depression. Maybe this book was given to you by a parent, teacher, school counselor, or other adult. Or perhaps you already know that you are depressed, and you're seeing a therapist who thinks the ideas in this book will be helpful to you. Chances are, if you're reading this, you or someone else has wondered if you're struggling with depression.

Within these pages we hope to help you to answer that question. We'll start with some basic information about what depression is. We'll also include some information you might find interesting about the role your brain and emotions play in making you depressed. Knowing what depression is and where it may come from will help you understand how depression can impact your life. It can help you recognize that depression can come from various sources, too—sometimes even more than one source at a time. While each person's experience is unique, we hope this information will help you recognize what you may be experiencing and also give you language to talk about it with trusted adults, should you decide to do so.

We are confident that having a better understanding of depression can help you to manage it, but this book is not meant as a substitute for getting professional help. Depression can make it difficult to follow through with making needed changes. Having a therapist as a sounding board and guide is important. And if you are feeling so down that you are having thoughts of suicide, it is urgent that you seek professional help right now. If you can't identify an adult to confide in, you can seek immediate help by telling your doctor, calling 911, or going to any hospital emergency room. See page 10 for more resources for preventing suicide.

HOW TO USE THE BOOK

Of course, if you're struggling with depression, you want more than to understand it. You want your depression to go away! Although we can't offer a quick solution, we will attempt to help you understand how behavior, thoughts, and emotions interact and catch you in a depressive loop. In addition to helping you see how this loop may make you feel stuck, we'll suggest some ways to interrupt it. Many of the ideas that are explained come from cognitive behavioral therapy (CBT). Research has shown this type of therapy to be effective in fighting depression.

Many kids who experience depression have the sense that it's out of their control—a roller-coaster ride that they can't get off. Maybe that's been your experience too. We hope to alert you to how the many decisions you make every day can make a difference in how things turn out for you. You may be surprised that a few important changes can make a gigantic difference in your emotional well being, in how you think about yourself, and in how you relate to the world around you. Our goal is to put you in charge!

Make a commitment to yourself. Learning and change of any kind is difficult. Overcoming depressed thoughts and behaviors doesn't happen overnight. Real change requires time and effort. For you to benefit from using this book, you will need to make a commitment to try new ways of thinking and behaving. Luckily, we have learned that taking 20 minutes or so most days to learn and practice the ideas presented here will make a big difference—a difference that lasts.

Read it. Of course it will be important to read the book, but we don't recommend starting at the beginning and just reading through to the end as if this is a textbook. Take your time. Read a section and then put it aside for a while. This pause will allow you to think about what you've read and begin to identify how the information relates to you. While the ideas aren't complicated, it can take time to observe how they are reflected in your life. Letting go of old habits and absorbing new habits into your life will happen gradually. Working slowly through the book will allow you to observe yourself in new ways and try different ways of thinking and acting.

Do the exercises. We've provided some quizzes, questionnaires, and exercises. As with the reading, you'll need to take some time to complete them and take note of how they may change you in smaller and then larger ways. If you are currently in therapy, your therapist may want to work on some of the exercises with you or even modify them to make them fit you and your situation.

Keep a journal. Reading this book will give you many new ways to understand and deal with depression, but we think a journal is an effective addition. Keeping a journal will help you become more aware of yourself. It will also allow you to plan and track changes you find useful and note the impact those changes have on your life.

And keeping a journal allows you to look back later at what worked for you. It helps you to mark progress, which will be a big boost to your confidence. As you proceed through this book, you can keep notes on the exercises you try and what you find most helpful or surprising when doing them.

SURVIVING THE RIDE AND LEARNING TO THRIVE

Life is like a roller coaster at times, but you can keep your balance by learning to identify behaviors and ways of thinking that impact your emotions in positive ways. You can cope with challenges if you learn ways to calm and refocus yourself. You can enjoy the ride when you learn to increase the number of successful experiences you have, become involved in fun and rewarding activities, build relationships with other people, set goals, and develop your personal strengths. The information in this book will help you learn strategies to protect yourself from having depression take control.

Journal Idea

Come up with a plan for journaling. Decide when you'll have time and energy to spend a few minutes focused just on you. Is bedtime a time when you can relax and think? Between school and after-school activities? Will you likely do better writing by hand or making notes on your computer or cell phone?

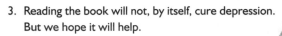

In a Nutshell

1. It's better to read this book in chunks to allow yourself time to think about the information presented and incorporate the ideas into new ways of thinking, acting, and feeling. Try not to just plow through the book as fast as you can in one sitting.

2. It's not necessary to do all of the exercises, but they are designed to assist you in developing new skills. Just as with building physical strength, building emotional strength takes practice over time.

3. Reading the book will not, by itself, cure depression. But we hope it will help.

CHAPTER 1

DEPRESSION AND TEENS

Depression is a word that's used quite a bit, but people don't always mean the same thing when they speak of depression. People may say that they're depressed when what they really mean is that they are sad. Sadness in the face of disappointment, loss, rejection, or other life events is a normal and necessary emotion. Sadness is a temporary reaction to something that happens, like when a friend says something unkind or you get discouraged about how you did on a test. Even when an event is tragic, like a death, sadness gradually lessens with time.

Depression is different. When a person is depressed, they are likely to experience other emotions such as guilt, humiliation, self-loathing, or anger as well as sadness. Depression tends to hang around or even worsen over time. For some people, depression may get better but then come back. While someone who is sad can point to a specific event that is leading them to feel that way, what causes depression may be harder to pinpoint. Sometimes depression can appear out of nowhere and the person experiencing it may not know why. Even if they can identify an event that set off the depression, their reaction may seem out of proportion to that experience. Or a depressed mood can hang around long after the event that triggered it has passed.

While everyone feels down at times, for some people, depressed feelings, thoughts, and behaviors can present serious problems. Depression can interfere with many basic areas of daily functioning—school, friendships, family relationships, routine activities, even just enjoying life. When this happens, the person is said to be experiencing a depressive disorder.

How do you know if what you are experiencing is normal sadness or a sign that you are depressed? A psychologist, other therapist, or physician can work with you to diagnose a depressive disorder. There are a number of different possible depressive diagnoses, depending upon your circumstances. Careful evaluation can be helpful in sorting out what types of treatments are likely to be most effective.

MORE ABOUT DIAGNOSES

There are several different depressive disorders, according to the American Psychiatric Association's *Diagnostic and Statistical Manual of Mental Disorders, Fifth Edition.* You can read about them in Appendix I at the end of this book.

Whether you have a diagnosable disorder or not, the aim of this book is to help you learn to feel, act, and think in ways that are healthy and effective. So what do you need to know to fight depression? Let's start with finding out more about the characteristics of depression.

Depression involves emotions. A person who is depressed may be sad, hopeless, defeated, anxious, insecure, irritable, feel worthless, or have other negative emotions. Or they may experience "the blahs," as if their sense of hopefulness or well being is just not there anymore. They may be bored with activities they used to find interesting. These emotions may come and go to a degree but they are more often present: They're there most of the day on most days, and may last for weeks or even longer.

Depression involves behavior. When someone is depressed, those emotions are internal, but the person probably also engages in depressed behaviors, which other people may notice. When a person is depressed, they may snap at others or become withdrawn. Grades in school may plummet because it's hard to concentrate or to get assignments done.

Depressive behaviors can include:

- Crying a lot or tearing up easily.
- Acting tired, with a loss of energy.
- Problems concentrating or paying attention.
- Difficulty making decisions.
- Sleep problems (sleeping too little or too much).
- Losing interest in activities.
- Losing interest in friends or no longer making the effort to be with them.
- Choosing new friends who have problems of their own.
- Staying alone in one's room.
- Showing little patience for other people.
- Losing one's temper easily.
- Changes in normal appetite (losing or gaining weight without trying to do so).
- Thoughts about death or suicide. (See the box on the next page.)

HELP IS OUT THERE!

IMPORTANT: ABOUT SUICIDE

Suicidal thoughts can seem like they will last forever—but they won't. No matter what you are struggling with, there are people who care and want to help.

We understand how painful life can be sometimes, and that you want the pain to end. Suicide is not the answer—**treatment is**. Teens who thought of suicide but were able instead to get help tell us that they are so glad they didn't kill themselves. When you are in crisis, it can be hard to see your way out. There are people who know what to do. Treatment works.

If you are thinking of suicide, it's important to recognize these thoughts for what they are: symptoms of a treatable illness. They are not true, and they are not your fault. Please tell someone right away.

You will be encouraged to create a Safety Plan, a list of steps you promise to follow during a suicidal crisis. It will include the names and phone numbers of people you can trust, people you can contact. It will remind you of actions that have helped you in the past and can help you now.

Know that you can get through this. Promise yourself that you will hold on for another day, hour, minute, whatever you can manage.

There are round-the-clock resources available if you need to reach out and talk to someone right away. You can call these hotline numbers:

National Suicide Prevention Lifeline: 1-800-273-TALK (1-800-273-8255)

The National Hopeline Network: 1-800-SUICIDE (1-800-784-2433)

You can also get more information online at:

http://www.suicidepreventionlifeline.org/

Depression involves thoughts. Although you probably already know something about depressive emotions and behaviors, it may surprise you to learn that depression also can include a certain way of thinking. These thoughts can be a result of depression but they can also reinforce depression when a person gets stuck in a confusing loop. When people are depressed, their thoughts often focus on unhelpful thoughts and overlook constructive ones. Repeated thoughts about problems or critical opinions about oneself are often a key feature of depression and are called "rumination." For instance, a girl who flubbed a line in the school play might think "I totally blew it and made a fool of myself" even if the mistake was hardly noticed by her audience. In a later chapter we'll explain different types of thinking that can occur with depression, and ways to interrupt the loop of depression.

WHY DOES DEPRESSION AFFECT TEENS?

As you no doubt know, your teen years are a time not merely of dramatic physical change but of social, emotional, mental, and role changes as well. As a teenager, you are faced with new responsibilities, a changing body, and competing expectations. While this rapid growth is all normal, it can also be extremely stressful. Perhaps it's not surprising, then, that there is an increase in depression when kids enter adolescence. Let's look at the range of biological and social factors that make teens more vulnerable to depression.

Did You Know? *You are not alone!*

At any given time, about 5 percent of teens are experiencing significant problems with depression. The rate is twice as high for girls as for boys.[1]

[1] Brent, D. A., & Boris, B. (2002). Adolescent depression. *New England Journal of Medicine*, 347(9), 667–671.

Hormones. You may have heard people say that hormones can wreak havoc with your mood, but why? It has to do with your brain. During the teen years, sex hormones tend to rev up the limbic system—the part of your brain associated with basic emotions. Brain imagery shows that during the teen years this system reacts more strongly to emotionally charged information than at any other time in our lives.

Both boys and girls have increases in testosterone during their teens. Testosterone increases a structure in the brain called the amygdala, which generates emotions of fear and anger—you know, the grouchys and grumpys! And people who suffer with depression tend to have a more active amygdala.

Did You Know? *Girls experience depression differently*

Girls may experience depressive symptoms cyclically in the week before their menstrual cycle begins. While for some girls these changes may be minor, for others mood changes can interfere with relationships and activities.

Brain development. Your brain is also in the process of developing, and its development is uneven. The pre-frontal cortex, the part of the brain that is in charge of calming emotional reactions and taking a cooler, more considered view of stresses, matures later than other parts of the brain. In fact, this area of the brain will continue to develop into your twenties! So the part of the brain that tells you not to overreact isn't fully online at the time when your limbic system is juicing up your reactions to stress.

Even the positive results of brain development can pose challenges in your teens. You may be aware that you can understand concepts and information that you couldn't grasp when you were younger. This leap in comprehension happens because the part of your brain that allows critical thinking is growing. But that critical thinking can be used against you. Teens are often most critical of . . . themselves!

> **CONSIDER THIS:** *If you believe that people should be treated with kindness and compassion,*
>
> *remember that you are a person and deserving of kindness and compassion.*

Body changes. Along with all these changes in brain and body chemistry come changes in your body itself. Adolescence is a time of tremendous physical growth. Most kids will be getting taller, and you may experience periods when your body slims down or plumps up. Bit by bit, as you transition from being a child to becoming an adult, the changes in your body shape and functioning can be a lot to adjust to.

As your body begins to develop adult sex characteristics (body hair, breasts for girls, larger muscles for boys, and so on), changes in body function (like erections for boys and menstruation for girls) can be challenging to get used to. You may have moments of anxiety or worry as you compare yourself to others or wonder if others are as aware of the changes that are happening to you as you are. You may have concerns about whether you are developing normally, and you may not be as confident about your body's appearance as you once were.

Rapid growth may also challenge you physically. For example, teens who are accomplished gymnasts may find floor routines more difficult as their bodies grow, which can be frustrating. Or previously well-coordinated teens may find themselves tripping over their newly enlarged feet! These rapid changes and new expectations can lead to struggles with body image.

New demands. Teens face extraordinary new demands and pressures. School demands increase, as do expectations to perform in other areas of your life like sports and extracurricular activities. If you're like most teens, you are facing questions and pressures about YOUR FUTURE. This pressure can include lots of questions about career goals, suggestions to make yourself look good for colleges, or messages that it's time to have experiences that may impact your chances of getting a good job in the future. You may be involved in a romantic relationship, which, while desirable, brings challenges as well. In other words, you've entered the stress zone!

One of the challenges you face in your teen years is developing a clearer sense of who you are. This process of becoming your own person involves developing your own sense of what you value. Taking greater control over the course of your life is also challenging. You have to make decisions about what changes you want to make in order to be more content, at peace with yourself, and fulfilled. You also need to be aware of what you can't change, and learn to accept those kinds of obstacles and move on despite them.

Cultural messages. As a teen you must contend with all of the media messages aimed at your age group. The social media, television shows, movies, magazines, and advertisements you consume every day contain hidden stressors you might not even be fully aware of. You are exposed regularly to hundreds of subtle (and not so subtle) messages about how you should look, what you should wear, what you should enjoy, what you need to do to be popular (and that popularity is important), what other people may be thinking about you, and what your life goals should be.

Let's face it: Many of the expectations these messages set are totally unrealistic. It's unlikely that any kid ever felt they were hitting a home run in all areas. Movie stars, musicians, athletes, and other "models" are presented in unrealistic ways. You rarely see them when they're ticked off (unless you are receiving a message that they're tough in a "cool" way), wearing dorky clothes, or doing things people wouldn't think fit the personality they are trying to portray. In fact, their presentation is carefully orchestrated by a whole team of publicity agents, stylists and make-up artists, clothing designers, photographers (armed with photo enhancement technology), and even people who do research on what teens think is cool. Unless you have such an army of professionals at your disposal, you'll never believe that you live up to the images they present. Lots of teens use these kinds of images as a measure of how they are doing in the world— BAD PLAN!

CONSIDER THIS: *Expecting perfection is a recipe for defeat. Even a good baseball player only hits the ball a third of the time.*

Through the media and through conversations with people you know, you may also experience pressure to identify yourself in a particular way. This coercion can take the form of suggestions to align with a label assigned to a social group in school (jocks, nerds, gamers, and so on). While identifying with a group can provide some sense of belonging, putting any type of label on yourself can be limiting. It may make you think you have to live up to expectations derived from those labels or keep you from trying new activities that don't seem to fit the identity you've been "assigned." You may be uncomfortable making new friends with a variety of other people. Or you may believe you need to give up old friends if your interests change.

RISK FACTORS FOR DEPRESSION

Some people are more vulnerable to developing a depressive disorder than others. While the reasons for this are not entirely clear, research has shown some factors that can put people at higher risk.

Life events. It may seem obvious, but not everyone faces the same life challenges. Sometimes uncontrollable life events, whether they are chronic or sudden and traumatic, can be overwhelming. If these experiences outpace your ability to cope, you may become depressed, despite your efforts to handle all you are experiencing. Or you may become so overwhelmed that you can't muster the energy to try.

Life challenges can include situations like family problems, health problems or an injury, a learning disability, or the loss of someone you love. Some kinds of changes, which are mildly stressful for adults, can be extremely difficult for teens. These include moving away from friends, changing schools, or an injury that disrupts a loved sport activity. Gossip, unwillingness to go along with the crowd, bullying, and difficulties with friends can also present real problems at this time in your life.

Family history of depression. You may have heard that people who have close relatives with depression are more likely to become depressed themselves. No one really understands the process fully, but it seems that some people may be genetically susceptible to depression. As with other kinds of genetic influences, just because someone in your family has been depressed doesn't mean that you inherited the genes that make you vulnerable. And, even if you did, genes alone don't cause depression. Other factors (such as stress, thinking style, capacity for coping, and so on) also have a significant impact on whether a person with a genetic predisposition actually suffers from a depressive illness.

CONSIDER THIS: *Genes, like jeans, impact how you look, walk, and act.*

Genes, like jeans, don't determine who you are.

Having a family history of depression can also make you more likely to become depressed for other reasons. If you live with people who have a habit of depressive thinking, they likely express it in the way they talk. Kids exposed to that kind of talk learn to think in depressive ways themselves. It might be informative to notice whether family members seem to be self-critical, make catastrophic predictions, refer to problems as more permanent than they really may be, or miss the positive aspects of their lives. Perhaps, unintentionally, your parents or other family members have spent years modeling ways of expressing themselves that resulted in your own tendency toward depressed thinking and unhelpful self-talk.

Personal history and stress. Difficult early life experiences or current life stress can increase the likelihood of depression in adolescents. These circumstances can include such extreme events as the death of a parent, a chronic disability, exposure to violence, experiencing neglect or abuse, or growing up in poverty. Less dramatic stresses that can increase the risk of depression include struggling with a learning disability, going through your parents' divorce, being bullied, or having a hard time making friends. For many teens who are gay or lesbian, bisexual, or transgender, lack of understanding or acceptance by those around them can make them vulnerable to depression.

LEARN TO IDENTIFY AND AVOID BULLIES

Being a victim of bullying raises the risk for depression. There are different kinds of bullying:

- Physical—kicking, hitting, or any use of aggression in order to control the other person.
- Verbal—use of "put down" language in order to hurt or humiliate the other person.
- Emotional—finding ways to isolate or shun the other person.
- Cyber—the use of instant messaging, cell phone text messaging, or online social networks to humiliate or embarrass someone.

While all forms of bullying are harmful, victims of cyberbullying report particularly high rates of depression.[2]

If you are being bullied, seek help from a trusted adult. You have a right to be physically and emotionally safe. Here are some additional online resources: http://us.reachout.com/ and http://www.stopbullying.gov/

Lack of light. Some people experience depression much more often in the winter, when the days are shorter and there is less daylight. Depression with a seasonal pattern seems to be triggered by changes in exposure to light with the seasons. Maybe you've heard about circadian rhythms, the body's internal clock. That clock is regulated by the sun. In the fall and winter, the body's internal clock may get derailed, interfering with sleep and contributing to depression. People with a seasonal pattern typically find that they improve when spring

[2] Wang, J., Nansel, T. R., & Iannotti, R. J. (April 2011). Cyber and traditional bullying: Differential association with depression. *Journal of Adolescent Health, 48*(4), 415–417.

returns and there is more daylight. For individuals with this kind of pattern, sitting in front of full-spectrum artificial lights can counteract the depression that occurs in the darker months. For some people, making an effort to be outside in the winter during daylight can also help. Your doctor or therapist can help you decide if light therapy may be indicated for you, and guide you in the best way to proceed.

Temperament. Babies are born with individual differences in how sensitive they are and how easily they can settle down when upset. You can see early differences in how active, vocal, and attentive babies are. Psychologists call this "temperament." Although the environment certainly modifies how these characteristics develop, it is clear that temperament is something you're born with. Some research suggests that babies who are irritable, fussy, and difficult to calm down are more likely to become depressed as teenagers. At the same time, experience can alter inborn temperament, and even those people with more reactive natures can learn ways to gain control over their reactions.

Teens with depression do not all experience the same symptoms. One may have trouble getting out of bed in the morning. Another may frequently reflect on perceived flaws, and yet another may experience sadness and hopelessness a lot of the time. But, in every case, depressed behaviors, thoughts, and feelings interfere with life. This book contains many specific tools and strategies for fighting depression. Even if you have risk factors for depression, you can overcome your biology, your experiences, and your environment to stay positive.

Journal Idea

After reading this chapter, are you aware of risk factors you have for depression? Make some notes in your journal about past or current experiences, biological risks, current stresses, cultural influences, and changes that come with being a teen that may be making you emotionally vulnerable.

In a Nutshell

1. Remember that there are three components of depression: thoughts, feelings, and behavior. Changes in any one of them can lead to improvements in the other two.

2. Several factors make teens more vulnerable to depression than people of other ages. Hormonal changes, brain development, body changes, increased expectations from others, and social and cultural pressures can increase the chances that a teen may struggle with depression.

3. Major risk factors for depression include biological factors such as genetics, past experiences and learning, traumatic events, and chronic stressors.

4. Having risk factors for depression does not automatically mean that you'll be depressed. Social support, coping skills, a positive thinking style, and other factors can override the impact of these risks.

CHAPTER 2

GETTING HELP

You probably don't have a lot of experience asking for help for how you feel and think. But you probably have had times when you needed help to learn something or to figure something out. In a way, seeking help for depression isn't that different. Getting treatment includes learning more about how depression works, how it impacts your life, and developing tools to overcome it.

SIGNS THAT YOU MAY NEED PROFESSIONAL HELP

Although we hope this book helps you to understand what depression is, where it comes from, and how to develop skills to fight it off, we know that some of the kids reading this will need more help than can be provided by a book. One in 20 teens suffers from a depressive disorder at some time. While there are lots of steps you can take that may prevent depression, having a depressive disorder does not mean you've failed. Some people develop a depressive disorder despite all their efforts to combat it. It's like doing everything you can to prevent getting a cold but getting one anyway. It's no one's fault.

Any time you get stuck thinking depressed thoughts, or if depression is interfering with your life or relationships, it may be time to seek help from a professional, whether you have been diagnosed with depression or not. So how do you figure out whether to seek help? On the facing page, there are some questions to consider. Ask your parents or another adult if you need help thinking about these questions. Some people who are depressed experience many of these issues, but some kids seek help when only a few of them are present.

HOW TO GET HELP

If the answers to some of the questions on the facing page are "Yes," it may be time to share what you're experiencing with a trusted adult. That's an easy thing to say but it can be hard to do. Telling someone about difficult emotions can be awkward or embarrassing. Some kids are unsure about whom to trust with such personal information, or worry that others won't be open to hearing about their depression. But chances are that if you've been struggling with depression, those around you have seen signs of it. Telling them what you're experiencing may help them to better understand why you've been acting as you have.

Whom to tell? Once you've decided to tell someone else that you're experiencing depression, the question arises: Whom should you tell? Most teens who are depressed naturally consider talking to a close friend first. If you have someone you can trust with this sensitive information, sharing your feelings might be a good first step. But whether you start by telling a friend or not, ultimately getting professional help will require reaching out to an adult.

Many teens who recognize they need help will first go to a parent. But, depending upon the circumstances of your life, you might find it easier to talk to a doctor, school counselor, teacher, coach, clergy person, or other adult whom you believe you can trust. Think about the adults in your life. Which of them will be easiest to talk to?

HELP IS OUT THERE!

IS IT TIME TO ASK FOR HELP?

- Have you experienced long periods of depression every day or nearly every day?
- Have you been struggling with depression for weeks? Months?
- Are there things you used to enjoy doing that you just have no energy for anymore?
- Does nothing grab your interest for long?
- Are you ashamed, embarrassed, or discouraged about yourself? Do you have the sense that you're just not worth it?
- Do you frequently feel a lot of guilt?
- Is it hard to concentrate on schoolwork when it didn't used to be? Have your grades dropped?
- Is it too darn hard to make decisions?
- Are you spending a lot of time alone? Avoiding time with friends? Spending time with new friends who make unhealthy choices? Avoiding your family?
- Are you having trouble sleeping even when you go to bed at a reasonable time? Do you lay there awake for an hour or more? Do you wake up in the middle of the night and have trouble going back to sleep?
- Are you sleeping too much or avoiding problems by sleeping in the daytime?
- Have your eating habits changed? Have you lost your appetite or lost weight? Are you binging on junk food to make yourself feel better or out of boredom?
- Are you agitated all the time?
- Are you tired all the time without reason?
- Do you find yourself annoyed with just about everyone?
- Are other people commenting that you seem down all the time, or are others acting worried about you?
- Do you think about death a lot? Do you have thoughts of hurting or killing yourself? Have you ever planned to commit suicide?

If you go to an adult other than your parents, they may encourage you to go to your parents next. Or they may ask if they can talk to your parents themselves.

CONSIDER THIS: *Often the blinders you wear keep you from seeing the helpers in your midst.*

A second look may reveal strong, caring supporters whom you've overlooked.

What does it say about you if you need help to deal with depression? Lots of kids avoid asking for help or even hide signs of depression because they are afraid of what others will think. Sometimes they think not being able to cope on their own is a sign of weakness. While these thoughts and emotions are common and understandable, they can also keep depressed teens from getting help. You are probably correct that many people won't understand. They may even be skeptical about seeking help for an emotional problem. But such prejudices are based on ignorance. Depression isn't a sign of weakness. It's an illness that, for an individual person, may have a complex set of causes, including genetics and environmental factors. Do not let other people's lack of knowledge keep you from seeking help.

THERAPY

You may already be seeing a therapist; they may be the one who told you about this book. If not, you may be wondering how therapy can help and what it would be like. Typically, teens see therapists by themselves (though group therapy or family therapy may be helpful in some cases). Your therapist will ask you questions about your experiences, emotions, and behaviors to help both of you understand how depression impacts you and the particular stumbling blocks it presents in your life. Your therapist may also interview your parents about what they see at home, but the therapist won't share what you say with your parents unless you okay it. They also won't share what you talk about with your school or anyone else. Your conversations and the specifics of your treatment plan are confidential. If your therapist thinks it would be helpful to involve others, they will first ask for your permission. There are some exceptions to this rule of confidentiality. Your therapist will seek others' help if they believe you are at risk of harming yourself, if they think you might injure someone else, or if they think someone else is hurting you.

What will therapy be like? Your therapist will make an assessment that might include making a plan to help with tangible problems that are contributing to your depression. For instance, if your depression was triggered by your being overwhelmed in school, they may see if you need help with academics. If family problems are affecting you, they may have ideas about that too.

After you and your therapist have gotten to know each other and they have some understanding of your depression, they will guide you toward addressing depressive behavior, thoughts, and feelings in much the same way as the remainder of this book does. Your therapist will help you to set goals and devise strategies to overcome unhealthy behaviors. They will help you to develop more realistic thinking to combat self-defeating thinking. It can be extremely helpful to have someone else work through these challenges with you. And sometimes just describing your experiences out loud can help to put things in a more realistic light. Your therapist can also serve as a coach to encourage you when you are having a tough time and to celebrate with you when you make progress.

CONSIDER THIS: *Knowing what you don't know is a sign of wisdom.*

*Being open to the guidance of others may open
your eyes to unexpected possibilities.*

Much of what psychotherapy can offer is a safe place with a trusted adult to talk about your thoughts, feelings, and behaviors, and develop ideas for dealing with them. Many of those ideas may be similar to the strategies presented in this book, but you'll have someone to talk to regularly about how to apply them to your specific situation, and someone who will check in with you about how you're progressing. And those talks will be ongoing and predictable.

Medication. Working with a therapist and using the types of strategies presented in this book may help a lot. But sometimes, even if you work very hard, it can be difficult to overcome depression. Your therapist may suggest that you add medication to your treatment plan. Research has shown that medication and therapy together can sometimes work better than either alone. Medication may help by lessening the intensity of your symptoms so that you have the energy and focus to follow through on treatment homework. While medication can be helpful, though, there's no magic pill that just makes depression go away. Instead, medication can make it easier to do the work that is needed to change the behaviors and thoughts that keep depression going.

This discussion may have you wondering what medication does. The brain chemicals serotonin and norepinephrine have been linked to depressive illness. Medications that impact these neurotransmitters, either by increasing them or slowing the brain's process of clearing them out, have been found to help in the treatment of depression. Once a psychologist or physician has evaluated you, they may suggest medication in addition to psychotherapy. If that happens, you will probably have a lot of questions you'll want to ask about the medicine itself. Questions might include:

- What should I expect the medicine to do?
- Will it make me feel weird inside or change my personality?
- Will I lose control?
- How long before it starts to work?
- What happens if I miss a pill?
- How do I explain to other people that I'm taking medication, and whom should I share this information with?
- What side effects might there be?
- What if I want to stop taking the medication?

Your doctor can answer any of those questions for you, so don't hesitate to ask.

You might also have questions about what it means to take medication. Some kids worry that deciding to take medication may mean that they're abnormal or inadequate in some way. In reality, taking medication in the context of treatment can be a mature and active decision to address a serious problem in a responsible way.

Other therapies that may help. Although they probably won't take the place of therapy or medication, if you're dealing with a significant depression, alternative treatments like meditation and acupuncture may help you to gain temporary relief from depression and the anxiety that may accompany it.

Other problems for which you may need help. As if having unwanted emotions weren't enough, depression can also occur with other kinds of problems. These are called "comorbids," and may require their own kind of intervention. While not everyone who experiences depression has comorbid problems, it's pretty typical for kids with the following problems to also be struggling with depression. If you find yourself dealing with any of these behaviors, it's likely you need to seek help:

- Anxiety that interferes with your life.
- Alcohol or drug abuse.
- Anorexia or bulimia.
- Cutting or other self-injuring behavior.

HELP IS OUT THERE!

SELF-HARMING BEHAVIORS

Behaviors in which teens intentionally hurt themselves can be associated with many different disorders, including depression. While there is an overlap in the methods of treatment of depression and deliberate non-suicidal self-injury, it is helpful to work with a therapist who has specific expertise with these behaviors.

Sometimes fighting depression requires a team, and a doctor or therapist or counselor may need to be part of the team. No matter who is on your team, they can help you to understand how depression takes hold.

In the next chapter, you will learn how to identify feelings, behaviors, and thoughts that influence one another in a loop of depression. Looking further ahead, in Chapter 4 you will discover that changes in your actions and activities can produce improvements in your thoughts and feelings. Chapter 5 will teach you how the ways you think can keep you stuck in a depressive loop and how changes in thinking patterns can stop the downward spiral. In Chapter 6, you will learn a number of problem-solving techniques, and in Chapter 7 you will learn coping skills for problems that don't have solutions. You will learn how to quiet your mind and calm your body in Chapter 8 with breathing exercises and relaxation methods. Chapter 9 asks you to look at and value your personal strengths as part of being a mentally healthy person. And then we're back to developing your "team" in Chapter 10 as you deepen and expand your relationships. Chapter 11 is a review of all the elements that will combat depression to help you get mentally healthy again.

Journal Idea

You can use your journal to have a "private conversation" with yourself about just how much you are struggling with depression right now. Do you think you could use the help of a therapist? What might be the best way, in your personal circumstances, to reach out for help when you are ready?

In a Nutshell

1. It's time to seek professional help if depression is interfering with aspects of your daily life, or if you get stuck and believe that nothing you do can make you better.

2. If you're thinking of suicide, you should not hesitate to alert a responsible adult or go to a hospital emergency room.

3. A trusted adult will likely be the best guide to getting treatment. Reach out to a parent, teacher, coach, or other adult to help determine the best source of professional support for you.

4. Treatment will start with an evaluation by a professional who may recommend therapy, medication, and/or other types of interventions. Effective treatment will require your active participation.

CHAPTER 3

THE LOOP OF DEPRESSION

Emotions are an important part of human nature because they give us information about our experiences of ourselves and others. The English language contains hundreds of words to describe emotions, yet many people struggle to understand why they think and feel the way they do. Learning to recognize your emotions and to put those experiences into words will help you navigate life's ups and downs.

UNDERSTANDING THE BRAIN-BODY CONNECTION

Your brain is constantly putting together all kinds of information, often outside your awareness. However, some information needs your attention. In certain situations, feelings in your body combine with past learning and experience to alert you to take action. One aspect of feelings comes from the signals in your body that are part of your nervous system. For example, sweaty palms, rapid heartbeat, and shaky knees are bodily sensations associated with fear. Fatigue, heaviness in your chest, and slow breathing may signal sadness. When you tune in to your body, you get some important clues to your emotions.

But an emotional response is much more than just physiological information. Your thoughts and knowledge help you make sense of your feelings. Even as you are making sense of your body's responses, your brain continues to work by contributing additional information about your own and others' motivations and actions, all within the particular context. You have a lot of information to process just to recognize your emotions, let alone put them into words.

While it is not necessary for you to understand the detailed workings of the brain, it is helpful to contemplate how complicated it is to know how and why you are experiencing particular emotions. You have choices about how you think about your feelings and about what to do given the situation at hand.

EXPERIENCES AREN'T THE SAME FOR EVERYONE

People are different in how they respond. Have you ever recommended a movie you loved to a friend only to have that person say they didn't like it? Or maybe you have a friend who enjoys hip hop while you prefer rock. People are also different in their emotional reactions to events. While some experiences can make just about anyone sad or down, some people seem to bounce back more easily than others. Why is that? A lot has to do with how a person thinks about an experience.

Take, for example, two girls who both try out for the lead in the musical at their high school. Both girls make it through two callbacks, yet neither gets the desired part. In fact, each one is asked to perform in only one group dance number. While each girl is disappointed, their different ways of processing their experiences result in remarkably different behavior and emotional reactions. One of the girls thinks "I can't sing at all! That's why I didn't get a part" and "I totally embarrassed myself by trying out in the first place!" That girl is so down she doesn't go to school the next day or talk to her friends about what she perceives as a failure.

The Loop of Depression

The other girl takes a completely different perspective. She thinks "That's too bad, but at least I get to be in the show. I'm sure they try to save the big parts for upperclassmen and I am just a freshman. I'll have other chances. I guess they liked my dancing, though, and this way I can hang out with my friends during rehearsals!" She was excited to go to school the next day and talk to everyone about the musical.

CONSIDER THIS: *Your reactions influence your outcomes.*

There's what happens and then there's what you make of it.

What each girl thinks to herself determines how she feels and what she does. This mutual influence of thoughts, feelings, and behaviors creates a loop.

THE THOUGHTS-FEELINGS-BEHAVIORS LOOP

Thoughts

Behaviors

Feelings

THE LOOP OF DEPRESSION

Your mood results from the ways you are thinking. When your thoughts are filled with hopelessness and self-criticism, you will perceive the world in a depressed way. Thus the loop of depression develops. You feel down, you think in unhelpful ways, and you withdraw. And what's worse, as the loop goes around and around, your feelings, thoughts, and behaviors may pull you in a downward spiral.

The good news is that an interruption in any part of that loop can provide opportunities for change. The loop can be interrupted by challenging depressive thoughts, by making small changes to unhealthy habits or depressed behaviors, or by letting go of sadness or anger about things that can't be changed. A change in one part produces change in each part. And, as you make changes, you may reverse the effect of the rotating loop as it starts to spiral in a more productive direction.

Here are some examples: Say your parents ask you to babysit your younger sister instead of attending the school dance. Consider some possible thought/feeling/behavior loops. You might think: "That's so unfair! I never get what I want." So you become upset and disappointed and argue with your parents. Alternatively, you might think: "That's so unfair. But maybe I can think of some fun things to do with my sister." You make make popcorn and watch a movie and actually enjoy an evening at home with your sister. Two different thoughts lead to different feelings and different behaviors.

Now let's try varying the behavior. Here's another event—soccer try-outs. You force yourself to try out, even though you feel tense and jittery, and you think "I hope I make the team." Alternatively, you avoid tryouts, thinking "I can't handle this," and you are relieved at first, but later you have regrets. What you do or how you approach a

Example 1: Your parents need you to babysit your younger sister, causing you to miss the school dance. If you are experiencing depressed thoughts, you might find that the loop looks like this:

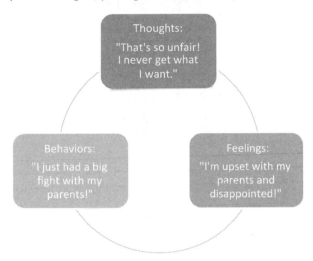

Example 2: But here's what the loop might look like if you react differently:

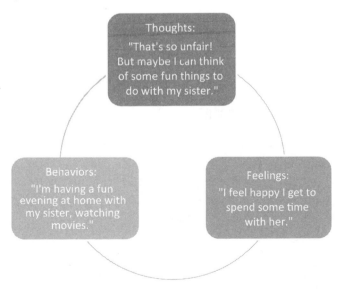

situation makes a difference in how you think about your experiences and in how you feel about them.

Your thoughts and behaviors in response to a feeling can also vary. For instance, if you overhear someone gossiping about you in an unkind way, you may feel hurt, but you can choose to ignore it and focus on other things rather than react and keep the loop going. If your pain causes you to think badly of yourself, you might lose confidence. Alternatively, if you hear the gossip and become angry, you might act in ways you will later regret.

The important point is that your feelings, thoughts, and behaviors are interconnected in a loop. Thoughts that are self-critical ("I'm so stupid") or that are lacking in confidence ("I'll probably fail") or that expect a negative outcome ("It'll probably get cancelled") will likely engender sadness or negativity that will, in turn, result in self-defeating or withdrawn behaviors. Those behaviors will likely cause depressed thinking and the feelings that go along with it. Likewise, those feelings will probably bring about self-defeating or withdrawn behaviors and depressed styles of thinking.

CONSIDER THIS: *Name calling is destructive and mean-spirited.*

Don't define yourself with unfair labels.

WHAT ARE YOUR TRIGGERS?

Some teens get stuck in the loop of depression—feeling down, thinking unhelpful thoughts, and acting in ways that keep them trapped in a depressive downward spiral. When this happens, it can seem like there's no exit. But there is. A cognitive behavioral approach is the preferred method for turning the loop around in a more positive and realistic direction.

The word "cognitive" refers to thinking and reasoning. When you learn different ways of thinking and different behavioral responses, your emotional experience will change. The first step is to recognize your typical thoughts, actions, and feelings. To do that, start by identifying your triggers. Triggers are situations or events that elicit certain thoughts, actions, or feelings in you. To recognize your triggers, think about the context of your experience of depression: What is happening? Where are you? Who else is there?

KNOW YOUR TRIGGERS

Rate how much each of the following would bother you on a 10-point scale from not at all (1) to very, very much (10).

RATING	TRIGGERS
	Three of your friends go out and they didn't invite you.
	You get a low grade on an exam.
	Your parents won't let you go to a party because they don't trust the host.
	One of your friends isn't returning your texts.
	You fail a class.
	Your outfit or your hair doesn't look right.
	You lose a game twice in a row.
	You break up with your girlfriend/boyfriend.
	Your girlfriend/boyfriend breaks up with you.
	Your parents criticize you for not doing a chore.
	Your brother or sister keeps taking stuff from your room.

These are all potential triggers. Something happens to set off thoughts and feelings. The things you rated a 7 through 10 are likely to trigger strong emotions. While you probably easily recognize those emotions, you may not be aware of your thoughts. For the most part, we are so used to our thought patterns that they are pretty automatic. But with practice you can learn to notice what you are thinking. Let's use some of the triggers listed to see what thoughts they might provoke.

Trigger: Three of your friends go out, and they didn't invite you. Even if this never happened to you, what might you think if it did? Don't go right to the emotion. Here are some examples:

"They are real traitors."

"I don't like them anymore."

"There must be a logical explanation."

"They don't like me anymore."

Trigger: You get a low grade on an exam. What might you think?

"That exam was too hard."

"I didn't study enough."

"I'm stupid."

"I hate that teacher."

Trigger: Your parents won't let you go to a party because they don't trust the host. Thoughts?

"They're probably right not to trust that guy."

"My parents are overprotective."

"My parents just want me to be safe."

"My parents are ruining my life."

Go through the rest of the triggers and generate possible thoughts. Do you notice any patterns in your thinking or does it depend a lot on the trigger? Do some seem more likely than others to start you thinking in negative ways? Certain types of thoughts are likely to result in depressed feelings and behaviors. That's how the loop of depression works. Something happens (a trigger) and you have the kinds of thoughts that set off depressed feelings.

THOUGHTS: THE CRUCIAL LINK BETWEEN TRIGGERS AND FEELINGS

You may know what types of triggers are easy for you to let slide and which you tend to be sensitive about. It may be much harder to identify the thoughts that often follow those triggers. Certain types of thoughts are more likely to result in depressed feelings and behaviors. If you can start to notice when you're having those thoughts, you can challenge them. The thing about these kinds of thoughts is that they can distort the way you see the world. Looking more closely at your thoughts will give you an avenue for evaluating your reactions, discovering more realistic ways to think about events and, most important, will point the way to an exit strategy from the loop of depression.

Your thoughts can be realistic or not realistic, helpful or not helpful. If your beloved pet dies, you may think about how much you miss them. It wouldn't be realistic or helpful to think that you don't care about their loss. And your thoughts may clarify how sad you are. Again, sadness is not bad or wrong. The goal is not to avoid your more uncomfortable thoughts and feelings. You need all of your emotions, not just the happy ones!

Be aware that sadness and depression are not the same. Sadness is a normal, even necessary human emotion. Depression is the outcome of a tangled loop of thoughts, feelings, and behaviors in

Did You Know? *Sad ≠ bad*

Mary Lamia, in her book *Emotions! Making Sense of Your Feelings,* explains that sadness helps you process your loss, signal others that you have a need for comfort, and alerts you to ways in which you may have to shift your goals or solve a problem.

which unrealistic and unhelpful thoughts create an unhealthy downward spiral. And depression often involves a variety of emotions, including guilt, shame, and anger.

As it becomes easier for you to identify your automatic thoughts, you will understand more about why you are experiencing particular emotions. And you'll see how your behaviors, while they make sense in light of your thoughts and feelings, are not necessarily healthy or useful. And, remember, with a cognitive behavioral approach, changes in behavior can also turn around the loop of depression, producing more realistic and helpful thoughts and manageable feelings. When you look at the behavior part of the process, note whether your behavior was healthy or useful and what happened as a result.

For example, think what would happen if your team lost a championship game (trigger). You say to yourself, "We would have won if I had blocked the goal" (thought), and you're filled with shame (feeling). You play video games all evening (behavior) and, since you go to school without having studied, you do poorly on a quiz (outcome).

Tracking your trigger → thought → feeling → behaviors → outcome cycle can teach you about yourself and whether you are thinking and behaving in a depressed way, resulting in a loop of depression. Use the chart on the next page to log your own patterns and gain self-knowledge.

The experience of depression can vary from person to person and from time to time. Observe your own depression-related thoughts,

MY EXPERIENCE LOG

Date/Time	Trigger	Thoughts	Feelings	Behaviors	Outcomes

feelings, and behaviors. What is the context? Here are some more
questions to ask yourself:

- Was there a specific event that triggered a loop of depression?
- Did you do anything that made you feel better?
- Did you do anything that made you feel worse?
- Did being in certain situations (alone or with other people, at
  home or out, busy or not) make you feel better or worse?
- Was there a time when you felt depressed but you were able
  to bounce back?

The steps to changing the loop of depression are doable. When
you are in a loop of depression, your thinking is irrational or unrealistic. Challenge those thoughts and you can redirect the loop, starting a new pattern of more productive thoughts. You will feel better
when you think in more logical and objective ways. And when you
feel better, you will be more engaged in the world and able to make
choices that boost your self-esteem and confidence.

Through keeping your experience log, you have learned what your usual triggers are and how some of your thoughts are distorted and self-defeating. As you read on, you will learn more about thinking errors and how to correct them and more about how to fight off depressed behaviors by choosing to do things that are helpful and healthy, even if you are reluctant. Breaking free of the loop of depression is possible, and it's worth it—and it's a set of skills that will last you a lifetime.

Journal Idea

At times when you experience depression, make notes about the circumstances that triggered that emotion and those that made it better or worse. Can you identify any depressive thought/feeling/behavior loops you engaged in today? Are there any portions of the loop that you could have changed? What might you have said or done differently? What unhelpful and inaccurate thoughts ran through your head? What feelings could you have let go of in order to have a more satisfactory outcome?

In a Nutshell

1. Whether an experience triggers depression depends not only on the event but also on your thoughts about that event, the feelings it arouses, and how you act in the face of that experience.

2. The loop of depression refers to the circular impact of thoughts, feelings, and behavior, which can both start depression and keep it going.

3. The loop of depression can be interrupted at any point in the cycle. This means you can make effective changes to thoughts, feelings, or behaviors that will modify depression in a helpful way.

CHAPTER 4
THE IMPACT OF YOUR BEHAVIOR

As you have learned, thoughts, feelings, and behaviors can all keep the depression loop spinning in a negative spiral. Remember that changes to any portion of the loop can alter it so it spins in a positive direction instead. In this chapter, we'll focus on ways you can change your behavior, which can result in more helpful ways of thinking and feeling.

DEPRESSED BEHAVIOR AFFECTS MANY ASPECTS OF LIFE

Depressed behaviors can occur in one or many parts of your life. Any or all of these behaviors are symptoms of depression that can fuel the depression loop.

Social behavior and depression. Is depression leading you to withdraw from friends, avoid social situations, or just not be pleasant to be with? Do you find other people too challenging or annoying? Or is the opposite true? Do you sometimes annoy people by being too clingy? Do you constantly need contact with friends and get overwhelmed by low moods when you are alone?

Does focusing on friends provide a brief emotional lift that doesn't last when the contact ends? Or maybe you are driven to become involved in other people's problems or conflicts. The adrenaline rush of their situations may seem better than the emptiness you experience when you are alone.

Family relationships and depression. While your family can be an important source of help and support if you are depressed, it can sometimes be difficult to be in close contact with others when you are not at your best. Parents' concerns about changes in your behavior may result in their asking questions about friends, school, or other aspects of your life that you don't wish to share. If they pick up on areas of your life that aren't going well, their concern can shine a light on things you'd rather ignore! Your own irritability may contribute to increased conflicts with parents and siblings. In many families, the more you try to avoid parental questions, the more parents may worry and the more likely they are to intrude.

Depression and school. A common symptom of depression is trouble concentrating. A lack of focus can occur because your energy level is low or because you are preoccupied with problems or with unwelcome thoughts and feelings. When you can't concentrate, school performance may slip. Troubles at school can add another burden of frustration, pressure, and self-criticism.

Depression and activities. If you're depressed, you may find it harder to be motivated for activities to which you have previously made commitments. That might lead you to drop a sport, music studies, volunteer work, or participation in a club. Or you may continue to participate but only half-heartedly.

Unhealthy behaviors. If you are depressed, you are more likely to engage in activities and behaviors that are unhealthy. Some of these—like spending too much time playing video games or on social media; tobacco, drug, or alcohol use; risky sex; or even shoplifting—can be misguided efforts to feel better. Others, like poor hygiene, staying up too late, not getting up in time for school, or not following through on responsibilities, can happen when you are overwhelmed by depression or are so drained by it that you find it hard to care about day-to-day concerns.

Depression and fun. You may find that, when you're depressed, fun just isn't *fun* like it used to be. There's even a specific word for this experience: "anhedonia." Anhedonia is simply the inability to enjoy things that were previously experienced as pleasurable and is one of the common symptoms of depression.

IDENTIFYING DEPRESSED BEHAVIORS

Not everyone experiences depression in the same way or acts the same way when they are depressed. Each teen who is struggling with depression will likely exhibit depressed behaviors in some but not all of the areas outlined above. Before you can change this part of the depression loop, you need to identify some of *your* depressed behaviors. Take a look at the list on pp. 46–47. It is not intended to be comprehensive but rather a way to help you begin to observe yourself. Take note of these and any other behaviors that you know go hand in hand with depression for you.

DEPRESSED BEHAVIORS

Check all that apply to you:

SOCIAL

☑ Not responding to friends' texts, emails, or other contacts.

☐ Making an excuse not to go out with friends.

☐ Acting grumpy or irritable.

☐ Losing friends or no longer being included in the "group" you used to be part of.

☐ Avoiding friends.

☐ Getting in arguments over silly things.

☐ Not seeing friends in the summer or over another school break.

FAMILY

☐ Blaming other people for your mistakes.

☐ Refusing to eat dinner with the family.

☐ Fighting with your siblings a lot (especially if you start it).

☐ Not responding when parents ask you casual questions about your day.

☐ Refusing to go on family outings.

☐ Regularly failing to complete household chores (especially if they were previously routine).

☐ Getting into fights with parents about getting up in the morning.

SCHOOL

☐ Having trouble concentrating.

☐ Frequently missing homework.

☐ Missing school (or skipping classes) or work when you are not sick.

☐ Wasting time playing video games when you know there are other things you should do.

☐ Procrastinating or struggling to start long-term school projects.

(continued)

DEPRESSED BEHAVIORS (*continued*)

ACTIVITIES

☐ Losing interest in sports practices or games.

☐ No longer spending time practicing an instrument or doing creative activities like you used to.

☐ Spending more time playing video games than engaging in other leisure activities.

HEALTH

☐ Engaging in risky behavior.

☐ Failing to shower or brush your teeth, or doing so only after parents bug you.

☐ Sleeping too little.

☐ Sleeping a lot in the daytime.

☐ Abusing drugs and/or alcohol.

FUN

☐ Being bored most of the time.

☐ Rarely laughing.

☐ Losing interest in movies, music, reading, or other activities you used to be really into.

☐ Finding most humor to be "stupid."

WHY WE DO WHAT WE DO (AND DON'T DO WHAT WE DON'T)

The types of behaviors discussed so far are not only symptoms of depression but can serve to keep you stuck in the loop of depression since they also contribute to depressed thoughts and feelings. For example, if depression contributes to problems concentrating in school, your grades may begin to fall. If your grades start to fall, you may begin to think that you're just no good at school or that you're a lazy person. And you may think even worse thoughts about yourself. One way to interrupt the depression loop is to begin to engage in more activities that support healthy thoughts and feelings. But first, a brief discussion about why we do what we do (and don't do what we don't).

The way people act is influenced by what happens as a result. For instance, if you regularly show up on time for an after-school job and work responsibly, your boss will pay you and might, eventually, even give you a raise. If that happens, it is likely to increase the chances that you'll show up for work and work hard in the future. This process is called "positive reinforcement."

POSITIVE REINFORCEMENT

Your behavior → Something positive and rewarding happens → Repeat your behavior

But there is another process called negative reinforcement in which your behavior is encouraged because something negative or unpleasant is removed. When you have upsetting feelings in certain situations, avoiding those situations spares you from the upset. In the same example as above, if your after-school job has some aspects that are frustrating, you might begin to avoid work, even though your boss will not pay you. This process is called "negative reinforcement."

REINFORCEMENT OF BEHAVIOR AND DEPRESSION

All behaviors, including depressed and healthy behaviors, are influenced by positive and negative reinforcement. If a behavior leads to something you like *or* helps you avoid or escape from something you don't like, you are more likely to repeat it in the future. Sometimes depression starts when you have tried to do something or get something and failed. For instance, having a best friend move away might make it hard to fill the social gap. If you then start to try to make a new close friend but can't seem to make a connection, you may stop trying and become depressed. Often, though, what starts depression can be hard to pinpoint.

Sometimes depressed behaviors can actually lead to positive reinforcement from others, such as when friends or parents are more attentive or concerned about you when you seem down. Less obvious, but maybe more important, depressed behaviors are often followed by negative reinforcement.

Depressed behaviors can start as a way to avoid or escape emotional pain. If you look back over the list of depressed behaviors earlier in this chapter, you may begin to see how many of them involve some type of avoidance or escape from experiences that are challenging, stressful, or unpleasant. Or depressed behaviors may result in pushing other people away, which reduces the social and emotional demands you have to deal with. Other depressed behaviors are a form of avoiding thinking about anything or distracting yourself from your emotions. Those experiences will then make it more likely that you'll repeat the behaviors, and you may enter a downward spiral of increasingly depressed behaviors that are, again, negatively reinforced by helping you avoid temporary emotional discomfort.

CHANGING THE BEHAVIOR EQUATION

Many depressed behaviors come hand in hand with depressed thoughts. But as you learned earlier, the loop of depression can be interrupted at any point. It's not necessary to be less depressed in order to act less depressed. By systematically changing some of your depressed behaviors, your mood will improve.

Another way that changes in behavior can alter depression is by adding new behaviors. By increasing healthy behaviors, you increase the likelihood that they will be reinforced. You will start to be more open to doing them (or less likely to avoid them). Healthy behaviors will then become easier, and it may be easier to let go of depressed behaviors. If depressed behaviors occur less often, they will be reinforced less frequently. In this way, small changes in behavior can help you interrupt the downward spiral of depression.

CONSIDER THIS: *We all get in ruts of unhealthy behavior.*

Commit to changing habits you know interfere
with your long-range happiness.

Changing depressed behaviors will require effort and a commitment on your part. After all, you will need to do things you don't really want to do, and at first it may be hard to accept the idea that *wanting* to do something can actually happen as a result of *doing* it. For this reason, we suggest that you start with small changes in behavior, giving yourself a chance to observe how this process works. Choosing which behaviors are likely to be helpful is very individual. You'll want to take care to select ones that matter to you and that are likely to be reinforced. Next, let's think about what matters to you so that you can set some behavior goals for yourself.

IDENTIFYING VALUES AND SETTING PERSONAL GOALS

As you start to think about what behaviors to change, remember that it's not important to *want* to do them. In fact, you probably *won't* want to at first. Choosing the first behaviors you are going to change will depend upon your spending some time thinking about what you really care about. Think about it this way: Rather than merely coping with whatever life throws at you, you can begin to become more active in shaping your life.

CONSIDER THIS: *Having goals can give you a sense of direction in life.*

Set goals for yourself that reflect who you are and who you hope to be.

You may have lots of people asking you about your goals. You know: "Are you hoping to get onto that team?" or "Where do you want to go to college? "or "What type of job do you want?" Those aren't the kinds of goals that we have in mind. While those may be objectives that you want to think about, you'll need to set some more personal goals: goals that will help to determine the type of person you will be and how you will spend your life.

When you think about your personal goals, your thoughts will reflect your values. Figure out your values and set goals from there.

Here are some questions that can help you clarify your values:

- What kind of person do I want to be?
- What do I want to give and receive in my relationships?
- How involved do I want to be in a community, and what types of communities matter most to me?
- What kind of environment do I want to live in?
- What activities give me satisfaction? What makes me feel like my time has been well spent?

For example, suppose that you know that when you get depressed, you often think you are being left out. Maybe you have lots of thoughts about why others seem to let you down or don't notice you. Maybe you've started keeping to yourself more to avoid a sense of rejection. While this might lessen the immediate hurt you feel, it doesn't help the real problem: You aren't satisfied with your relationships. If that's the case, it suggests that it's important to you to have meaningful connections with other people. In that situation your *goal* would be to interact more with others in a way that helps you become more connected. The goals you choose will be based upon values that are important to you and could include things like:

- I value being smart and well-educated.
- I think it's important to be responsible and reliable in a job.
- I value friendship and want to be a good friend.
- I think it's important to take care of my health.

Stating your goals in those ways does not make it clear what behaviors you might change. You still need to consider the small

DO YOUR BEHAVIORS FIT YOUR VALUES?

After thinking about how depression may be impacting your behavior, think about how depressed behaviors may be interfering with what you really value. Consider each of the areas of behavior discussed earlier in this chapter: social, family, school, activities, health, and fun. Do your current behaviors in each arena fit with the way you would like to be? Are they interfering with how you would like to be living your life now or in the future? What is one personal goal that really matters to you?

behaviors that could move you baby step by baby step closer to your personal goals.

FROM PERSONAL GOALS TO BEHAVIORS

Once you have a sense of what is important to you, you'll need to spend some time focusing on specific behaviors that could help you to reach your personal goals. Ask yourself how behaviors related to your goals might be different if you weren't depressed, or how you acted before you became depressed. These questions may help you to identify some behaviors to pay attention to.

At this point it's best to include as many as you can. In the example above of wanting to be more connected to other people, you might include objectives like:

- Smiling at other people.
- Saying hi.
- Inviting someone to a movie.
- Offering to help someone with homework (or asking for help).
- Joining a club or sport team.
- Asking to sit with a group at lunch.
- Starting a conversation.

- Hanging out after school.
- Attending school sporting events.
- Going to a school dance.

CONSIDER THIS: *Knowing what you want sets the path.*

Being willing to take steps forward moves you toward your goals.

Some of the behaviors on your list may seem too difficult at first. These can be saved until you've attempted some of the easier ones.

GOAL BEHAVIORS THAT SUPPORT MY VALUES

Easy	Harder	Even Harder	Hardest

None of the goal behaviors will result in immediate success. What's important is to start moving toward your goals: to take action. The particular action you take matters far less than taking some action.

BEING PROACTIVE

It's not enough to have a list of behaviors that could help you to reach important goals; you need to actually do them. And you need to do them often enough and persistently enough so they can work. This means being proactive. In order to be proactive, you need a plan of action and a commitment to yourself to follow through with that plan. As a proactive person, you don't just deal with what the world hands you; you take your life in hand!

CONSIDER THIS: *No one plans to fail but lots of people fail to plan.*

Plan for the change you want.

Your proactive plan will need to break down your values into goal behaviors you can do and monitor. Be specific when choosing those behaviors, and make sure the behaviors you start with are small. A behavior like "be friendly" is both overwhelming and unclear. A better behavior to start with might be "Give someone a compliment" or "Smile at three people on the way to class."

Making progress by being proactive requires you to stick with your plan over a long period of time, not expecting to fix everything immediately. Once you have a goal (or several goals) in mind and have identified small behaviors that may help you to move toward your goal, start setting daily objectives to incorporate into your life. Start with the easiest behaviors on your list. The harder ones will seem more manageable after you have some successes—even if they're small ones.

Taking action to make desirable changes in your life is empowering. Small changes can often make a big difference. When you identify depressed behaviors and work toward countering those with steps in a better direction, you will see a difference in your thoughts and feelings as well. Positive reinforcement of healthy behaviors will make them easier to continue. The thought-feeling-behavior loop begins to spiral in an upward direction when you take action that moves you, objective by objective, toward goals that matter to you.

TRACKING YOUR PLAN AND THE IMPACT OF BEHAVIOR

Tracking what happens to your behavior as you begin to be more proactive can be helpful. Use a chart like this one to note your planned behaviors. Each action can be rated (on a scale of one to 10) afterward for how much you enjoyed it (the mood it created) and to what extent it gave you a sense that you had some control over your life. You can keep these notes in your journal so you have a concrete record of your progress over time.

Date:____

Planned behaviors of the day:	Check if done	Enjoyment rating	Control rating
1. _____	_____	_____	_____
_____			
2. _____	_____	_____	_____
_____			
3. _____	_____	_____	_____
_____			
4. _____	_____	_____	_____
_____			
5. _____	_____	_____	_____
_____			
6. _____	_____	_____	_____
_____			

(Rating scale: 1 = none, 5 = pretty good, 10 = wow!)

Journal Idea

What behaviors are you aware of that signal that you are becoming (or already are) depressed? What small changes can you make that can move you closer to your personal goals? Are you ready to make those changes? Remember that one small but important change you can make this minute is to make a written commitment to yourself to take these small steps toward becoming healthier.

In a Nutshell

1. Depressed behaviors can increase the likelihood that you'll have depressed thoughts and feelings, which may end up interfering with your daily functioning and with your relationships.

2. Change your behavior in order to change your mood. Take action even if you don't feel like it.

3. Set goals based on your values. Think about what's important to you. Goals give you direction.

4. Break goals into manageable steps in order to encourage yourself to keep moving forward. That's called being proactive.

CHAPTER 5
THE IMPACT OF YOUR THOUGHTS

Remember, in addition to making changes in your behavior, you can also interrupt the loop of depression by making changes to your thinking. Certain types of thoughts frequently result in depressed feelings.

WHERE DOES DEPRESSIVE THINKING COME FROM?

Many kinds of frustrations, failures, and disappointments can make you more vulnerable to future depressive thoughts. If someone hurts your feelings, if you are separated from friends and family, or if you have experienced the loss of someone you are attached to, you are likely to be experiencing loneliness. Loneliness can distort your interpretation of how others are treating you and make you jump to incorrect, and hurtful, conclusions.

Experiencing failure may also make you prone to depressive thinking. When you try to achieve a goal but don't, you may start to tell yourself that you can't. This response to failure is especially likely if you've tried repeatedly, or if the goal seems an easily attainable one. If you begin to tell yourself that further effort will just lead to more letdown, chances are you'll be less likely to try again. These kinds of "I can't" thoughts can spill over to other things you want to do. Or they might start you thinking of yourself in ways that will actually block your progress. You might even begin to call yourself destructive and discouraging names.

Depressive thinking can come from your surroundings. For example, some families or peer groups have a tendency to express negativity. When you hear such messages repeatedly, you incorporate this type of thinking, even if the statements have nothing to do with you. Some examples of these kinds of depressive thoughts are "I'll probably lose my job" or "Things never go right around here." When the people you hang out with are saying "This school is the worst" or "What's the point of trying?" over and over again, you can be drawn into their belief system. You can begin to think in depressive ways when you are bombarded with media that may emphasize hopelessness and failure. Fortunately, you can learn to become aware of unhelpful ways of thinking and resist depressive thoughts and self-statements.

The first step is to identify depressive thoughts.

CONSIDER THIS: *"Can't" robs you of hope.*

Consider how you "can" see things in a hopeful way.

IDENTIFYING TYPES OF DEPRESSED THOUGHTS

This kind of thinking isn't something you have to accept. If you can start to notice when you're having depressed thoughts, you can challenge them and make changes to your inner "self-talk." Depressed thoughts can distort the way you see the world. With that in mind, we don't suggest that you merely tell yourself that they're not true or substitute an empty-sounding pep talk but rather bring them out in the open. Challenge their accuracy, and consider whether there's a less destructive and MORE REALISTIC way to think about things.

Depressed thinking can distort your view of the world in a variety of ways. The first type of distorted thinking we're going to discuss is "all or nothing" thinking.

"All or nothing" thinking. Often our depressive thoughts are overly general. This is sometimes referred to as "overgeneralizing" or "global thinking," because such thoughts involve taking a specific negative event (WHAT) that happened with certain people (WHO) in a certain situation (WHERE) at a certain time (WHEN) in a given way (HOW) and presuming it applies to all "WHO, WHAT, WHERE, WHEN, and HOWs." "All or nothing" thinking oversimplifies your thinking in a way that leads you to tell yourself stories about yourself and your experiences that are only partly true.

If you focus too much on events that fit into a hurtful or self-critical story about yourself, it's easy to overlook positive experiences that don't fit that narrative. If you think a negative experience will happen repeatedly, you may miss evidence that it hasn't happened in other circumstances. If you tell yourself that it happens everywhere, you may forget situations where it hasn't or won't happen. If you think an upsetting situation or event will last forever, it's much more likely to lead to depressed feelings or behaviors than if you think it will pass in time. If you keep focused on how it happened, you might be less focused on how to do things differently.

CONSIDER THIS: *What you tell yourself*
can be encouraging or deflating.

Choose the stories you tell yourself carefully.

Be aware of what you tell yourself at times when things don't go your way. When you are struggling with feelings of depression or when you notice that you're losing sight of important goals (or exhibiting depressed behavior), examine your thoughts carefully. Go through the "WHO, WHAT, WHERE, WHEN, and HOW" of the situation and ask yourself if the stories you are telling yourself might be too limited or self-defeating. There a few word cues that might signal "all or nothing" thinking.

- WHO—Do your thoughts include words like "everyone" or "no one?"
- WHAT—Are your thoughts full of negative words about yourself ("dumb," "fat," "awkward," and "loser" are examples)? Are you giving yourself labels that are permanent and unchangeable? Are you calling yourself names that you'd never consider using to refer to a friend?
- WHERE—Are you thinking "everywhere" when "in this situation" is more accurate?
- WHEN—Words like "this time" may be truer than "always" or "never."
- HOW—Is it really in "all ways" or just "this way" that things didn't go well?

Let's consider an example. A girl goes to the school dance and no one asks her to dance. She might initially experience these WHO, WHAT, WHERE, WHEN, and HOWs: Guys don't like me. I'm such a loser. I'm through with dances. No one will ever ask me to dance. All the other girls danced with a guy. That was the worst night of my life.

Sounds pretty dismal, doesn't it? Consider how these alternative thoughts might lead her to a different understanding:

Original Thought	Alternative Thought
Guys don't like me.	A lot of guys I know didn't come to the dance.
I'm such a loser.	When the girls and I were dancing together, Charlene did compliment my moves.
I'm through with dances.	I do like to dance.
No one will ever ask me to dance.	Someone will probably ask me to dance and if they don't, I can ask a guy to dance.
All the other girls danced with a guy.	Nikki, Grace, and Maya didn't dance with guys either.
That was the worst night of my life.	The music was good and my outfit was awesome.

Keep in mind that the goal isn't pretending or just turning a negative into a positive. It's okay to be disappointed about an experience. The goal is to catch your thoughts when one thing that doesn't go well starts to grow and take over the entire experience. Challenging your "all or nothing" thoughts can help you to limit the disappointment to what really went wrong (which probably wasn't everything!). Eventually, you may be able to change your habitual thought pattern from automatic global negativity to a more specific, more realistic thought process. After all, the alternative to "all or nothing" thinking is to find some middle ground.

Being alert to the "WHO, WHAT, WHERE, WHEN, and HOW" of depression can offer insights into strategies for interrupting the process.

"All or nothing" thinking isn't the only type of thinking that can distort your view of the world and get you trapped in a depressive cycle. Some other kinds of depressed thinking include:

Categorical thinking. As humans, our ability to put things into categories helps us to simplify the way we see the world and to make sense of it. But thinking about other people or yourself in categories that are too restricted can be limiting and distort your experiences. If you view yourself as fitting into certain categories too exclusively, you may be upset if you sometimes don't fit into that box. If, for instance, you see yourself as "nice," you may feel more than an appropriate amount of shame for doing something unkind. Or if you view yourself as a model student, it may be hard to admit to parents, teachers, or yourself when you are having trouble with a class.

Categorical thinking can also result in becoming overly let down when others don't do "what they are supposed to do" (based upon expectations of the category you've placed them in). For example, expecting teachers, parents, coaches, or other adults in authority to be perfectly fair can set you up for extreme hurt when they are not.

Expecting that friends should always stick up for each other may lead you to think you have no friends at times when they overlook you.

"Shoulds." "Shoulds" are a kind of categorical thinking that comes from very strong beliefs about the way the world is supposed to be. If you tend to have a very strict sense of what is right and wrong and how you and others should behave in certain situations, you may be vulnerable to "should" thinking. This can include being unforgiving when you or someone else makes mistakes, believing you always have to do your best, and fitting certain expectations all of the time. Do you find that you are often telling yourself you should be able to do something or that you should have done something? Would you be better off being less of a hard taskmaster and more realistic about how much you can do? Do you become overly frustrated when others do things you think aren't right? Is it hard to move past those experiences? Maybe it's time to question whether the "shoulds" running through your mind are serving to help you or harm you!

"Shoulds" can also refer to expectations of other people or reflect unrealistic expectations of perfection from the world in general. If your beliefs that life should be fair, people should be reliable, or hard work should result in positive outcomes are held too rigidly, you may feel betrayed and defeated when you encounter experiences that don't reflect those beliefs.

Focusing on the negatives and failing to see the positives. Some people tend to be more attuned to the bad things that happen to them than to the good. Or, when something happens that has both good and bad aspects to it, they may see only the bad. If you find that you often complain (aloud or even just to yourself) about all the bad things in life, you might want to consider what positive things you may be overlooking. Again, this isn't the same as ignoring the negatives. It means being sure that you give at least equal attention to the positives so that you ultimately come away with a more balanced and realistic viewpoint. Do you ever focus so much on your parents putting limits on the use of electronics that you fail to think about the fact that they buy you electronics? Have you ever felt totally bummed by having to stay home and do chores instead of hanging with your friends? Do you remind yourself that having friends who are cool to hang with is a big plus in your life?

Selective negative memory. Selective negative memory is somewhat similar to focusing on the negatives but involves rewriting history. It's normal for memories to become changed and only partially recalled over time. If the stories you repeat to yourself start to morph in a negative direction, or if you tend to spend a lot of time thinking about past experiences that you found painful, you may be increasing your overall sense of depression. Sometimes this tendency to remember events and situations in a negative light can take hold when you are down. Without your trying to do so, you may begin to search for evidence from past experiences that back up your negative impressions. In time, you may actually change your memory of those experiences. If you often engage in selective negative memory, you may soon find you've developed a life story of past failures, hurts, mistreatment, and disappointment that changes your experience of your present. For example, if a new acquaintance isn't as responsive to your efforts to get to know them as you like, comparing their behavior to that of a friend who betrayed you in the past will probably make you want to stop trying to be friendly.

Emotional reasoning. "Emotional reasoning" refers to depending too much on emotions and not enough on reasoning. This thought pattern can include jumping to conclusions about reality based on your emotions—that is, deciding that something is true because it "feels that way." For example, if you are nervous about attending a club meeting, you assume it's a bad idea to attend, or if you feel uncertain about your comment in class, you assume what you said is wrong. Do you find yourself saying (or thinking) that there are things you "just know"? As you read this book, you will likely get a clearer sense of how making judgments about reality based on your initial gut reaction may be unwise and unhelpful. If you are depressed, the chances are that your "gut reaction" is causing you to view the world through an inaccurate lens.

Personalization. Do you find yourself thinking "It's all because of me" when something goes wrong? Although it's important to admit to mistakes that you make along the way, you'll find life difficult if you overestimate the degree of control (and therefore responsibility) you have over disappointing outcomes. Personalization can also include a sense that others are aware of you and everything you do. Does it ever seem like your parents' arguments over money are because they are trying to save for your college? While trying to pay for college may be high on their list of goals, adult financial stresses rarely come from only one source. Did you ever think that a coach's lecture about needing to step up the effort out on the field was directed your way? It takes a team to win or lose a game. If you often view events in this way, you may tend to "personalize" others' frustrations.

Mind reading. Assuming you know what others are thinking about you without real evidence is called "mind reading." Teens are often very self-conscious as well as self-critical. When you identify something you dislike about yourself or your behavior, you may assume that others have the same thoughts about you that are running through your own head. It's very unlikely that anyone else is paying as close attention to your missteps as you are. Many "faults" that you see in yourself or in what you do may not be apparent to those around you. In fact, if the viewer is another teen, the chances are they may be too focused on their own insecurities to notice!

Distorting how others view you may increase your sense of insecurity, shame, and embarrassment. It may also contribute to your withdrawing from those people you presume see you in a negative light, making it harder for you to see signs that this may not be accurate. For instance, if your teacher calls you out for talking to a friend during class and you become convinced that that teacher "hates" you, you may be trying to read their mind. You may also avoid that teacher and miss the fact that they think you are incredibly organized. Or if a friend of a friend isn't friendly to you and you decide that they don't like you (when the truth may be that they are shy or distracted), this is also mind reading.

Magnifying and catastrophizing. When something goes wrong, do your anxieties tend to snowball? Do you tend to take a single experience and project it into the future with increasingly negative consequences? If you engage in catastrophic thinking, you may convince yourself that what is happening in the here and now will lead to devastating future consequences. If so, you are engaging in "magnifying" thoughts, taking a problem and making it grow larger and more overwhelming. Taken to an extreme, this kind of thought distortion can lead to "catastrophizing," as you imagine a terrible possible outcome and begin to believe that it is inevitable. This kind of destructive thinking can come into play when you are thinking about your future and how certain events now will inevitably interfere with your chances of getting into a good college, having the career you want, or being successful in the future.

What's the point? Some teens just give up before they even try to think things through. This can happen when you define a problem in a way that implies there are no possible solutions, ways around it, or options. This kind of thinking can throw a roadblock in the path of solving problems and actively coping. For instance, if you think "No one likes me," you may give up trying to make social connections. Or if you tell yourself "I'm no good at physical stuff," it's unlikely that you'll try new sports or other physical activities, and you may never discover one that you enjoy.

If you find yourself engaging in any of these kinds of depressive thinking, first of all, good for you for recognizing that. Noticing these thoughts isn't easy (though you will get more skilled at it with practice)! But then you have to take the next step to challenge these thoughts. Look for evidence that may contradict them.

CHALLENGING DEPRESSED THINKING

Consider this example:

Joe blew his Chem test. He was really upset because his grade wasn't up to par even before this exam (he thought he *should* be able to get a certain grade). Joe started to worry that his final grade for the class would be bad. His teacher and parents would be disappointed (a bit of *mind reading*), and he'd lose his edge in applying to colleges. In fact, he'd probably not get into a "good" college (a little *categorical thinking* going on here). And if he didn't get into a good college, he wouldn't get a good job. If he didn't have a good job, he might not be able to support himself (whoa . . . slow down, Joe, *catastrophizing* is taking you down a very bad road!).

If Joe could catch some of his depressive thoughts and consider whether they were really true or not, he might be able to interrupt the downward spiral that started with getting a bad grade. He could have:

- Reminded himself that there was still time to pull his grade up.
- Remembered that everyone (even his teacher and parents) knew that this was one of the toughest classes in the school and also knew that he was working hard to do his best.
- Focused a bit on the classes he was doing well in, not just the one he was struggling with.
- Done a bit of research on colleges—the ones that are hardest to get into aren't the only "good" colleges around. And by the way, "good" students don't always achieve a perfect record.
- Told himself that one grade, in one class, on one day was not likely to impact the entire rest of his life.

When something happens that triggers a depressive reaction, stop and examine the types of thoughts you are having. If you can begin to recognize some of the thought distortions discussed earlier in this chapter, you can begin to challenge them.

Ask yourself:

- Am I telling myself that this always happens when it only sometimes happens?
  - Seeing a problem in a more specific way may help you see specific solutions, or at least help you keep in mind that a negative event is temporary, only part of your life, and doesn't involve everyone who is important to you.
- Am I using permanent, negative labels to describe myself rather than thinking about a particular behavior at a particular time?
  - Don't let your weaknesses or moments when you're not your best define who you are. You are a complex individual with a combination of strengths and weakness who experiences good times and hard times.
- Am I missing the positive things I do or have and giving too much weight to my weaknesses, mistakes, or unfulfilled wants?
  - Don't overrate the bad times or fail to celebrate the good ones. Be sure to give yourself credit for your good qualities and behaviors.
- Do I remind myself repeatedly of past situations that upset me and fail to recall my prior successes and pleasures?
  - Learn from past mistakes but then be willing to let them go.
- Are my emotions overriding my reasoning? Might focusing on evidence of what is really true prove my initial impressions were unwarranted?
  - Truth doesn't live in your "gut." Your first reaction to an event may be a complicated mixture of reality, anxieties, distorted thinking, and fears. Check out other possible explanations and interpretations for events that make you upset.

- Are there factors outside of my current control that resulted in a negative outcome?
  - Taking responsibility for your mistakes matters a lot, but it's equally important not to think you are responsible for things over which you have no control.
- Might I be jumping to conclusions about the opinions others may have about me?
  - Although you may be acutely aware of your every misstep and error, it is unlikely that others are. If you believe that someone important to you has a problem with you, consider checking it out by asking them about it.
- Am I too rigid in my expectations of myself to be perfect? Am I too harsh when others disappoint me?
  - No one can be "on" or do their best all the time. Learn to forgive yourself your imperfections and forgive others for theirs.
- Do I tend to worry about how one problem might lead to later problems or even to dire results?
  - When you catch yourself "growing a problem" into a larger one, insist to yourself that you need to stop and keep your perspective. Consider that your situation could improve or even go better than expected. Try to think about what you could do to increase the likelihood of a positive outcome and decrease the likelihood that things will get worse.
- Do I use language that makes a problem seem insurmountable so I give up before I even try to solve it? Do I tell myself I just can't deal with something instead of actively helping myself get through hard times?
  - Try describing a problem in a different way—a way that suggests actions you can take that might lead to solutions. Take active steps to cope and take care of yourself.

PRACTICE REFRAMING DEPRESSIVE THOUGHTS

Spending some time thinking through alternatives to depressive thoughts can really be a great way to become more self-aware and help you make important changes. Write down any distorted depressive thoughts you have become aware of. Ask yourself if you're focusing too much on the negatives. Challenge yourself not to read minds, not to take things personally when they aren't personal, and not to think of all the snowballing negatives ahead that may make you assume that disaster is inevitable. What alternative, more accurate thoughts can you think of?

Depressive thoughts   More helpful and accurate thoughts

_____   _____

_____   _____

_____   _____

_____   _____

_____   _____

When you begin noticing unhelpful patterns of thinking and you work actively to find alternative thoughts, you will find that your emotions change too. They will be less extreme. And when you are less upset, you will be more equipped to address problems, find solutions, and engage in worthwhile activities.

THINKING ABOUT THINKING

Have you ever had a song stuck in your head? Most people have experienced this kind of temporary repetition of a catchy tune that eventually goes away. In the same way, people think all kinds of thoughts, some of which are welcome and make sense—and some not so much. Depressive thoughts can also replay over and over again in your head in an unhealthy way. Becoming aware of these repetitive thoughts can be a first step toward reducing their impact on your mood. Just as you tend to notice that a song is stuck in your head and not just focus on the lyrics, you can begin to notice the process of thoughts getting stuck in your head. When this happens it's called "rumination."

You may believe that by focusing on a worry or problem you will find a new way to deal with it, prepare for the future, or solve it. Unfortunately, rumination more often results in unproductive thinking and depressed emotions. You may also believe that this is something over which you have no control: "It just happens" or "I can't stop it." While changing the way that you think is challenging, it's not impossible.

Telling yourself to "stop thinking about this" probably won't work. In fact, it might even make it harder to stop. Instead, try giving yourself messages to become less involved with the thoughts. Step away from them in a way that makes them less meaningful and important. Have you ever done the speech exercise where you repeat the phrase "toy boat" over and over again at a faster and faster pace? If not, try it now. As you do so, the words, which at first had a clear meaning, begin to be harder and harder to say until it seems that you are saying meaningless sounds instead of words. In effect you have stepped away from the words as words and turned them into objects that no longer have the same meaning for you. Another way to understand this is that you have become "detached" from the content of the words. With practice you can learn to detach from your ruminating by stepping away from the meaning of your thoughts and letting them flow through your mind without meaning. This is called "detached mindfulness."

Let's take an example. Maybe a friend's behavior has hurt you, and that experience triggers a thought track like a song stuck in your head. You become aware of a number of depressive thoughts that you've run through your mind many times in the past. You could:

- Become aware that the thoughts are playing in your mind.
  - "There goes that soundtrack putting me down and making me worried about my social life."
- Decide that you don't want to get wrapped up in those thoughts.
  - "I'm not going to get wrapped up with this story."
- Allow the thought to be there and run its course without trying to push it away or make sense of it.
  - "The thoughts are going to happen and then they'll go away. There's nothing to be gained by thinking this through and nothing to be learned here. This is an outdated, boring old song!"
- Decide to put off being concerned about this until later in the day or even tomorrow.
  - "It's not helpful to try to deal with this right now since these thoughts will lead me down a depressed road. If they're really important to focus on, I can do so later and, if they're not, I'll just let them pass by."

Becoming aware of depressed thinking patterns can be challenging. Often that type of thinking is automatic, and happens rapidly. At the same time, these thoughts can have a tremendous impact on how you experience the world around you, how you feel, and how you act. Catching yourself in the act of depressive thinking will allow you to take corrective action by challenging thought distortions. You then have an opportunity to replace depressive thoughts with healthier and more realistic ways of thinking.

Journal Idea

As you begin to become more aware of depressed "lyrics" that you play repeatedly, see if you can give them titles. Chart what triggers them, whether you were able to disengage from them, or if you successfully put them off for a while. Over time, note whether those depressed "songs" begin to play less often or lose their meaning.

In a Nutshell

1. Depressive thinking involves a distortion of reality. Its opposite is realistic thinking.

2. "All or nothing" thinking, categorical thinking, focusing on the negative and missing the positive, selective negative memory, emotional reasoning, personalization, mind reading, "shoulds," magnifying and catastrophizing, and thinking "What's the point?" are all forms of distorted thinking that can be associated with depression.

3. Since depressed thinking involves untrue distortions, you can challenge those thoughts with more accurate thoughts.

4. Rumination refers to unhelpful thoughts that repeatedly run through your mind. You may not be able to shut them off, but you can change how important they seem by practicing detached mindfulness.

CHAPTER 6
EFFECTIVE PROBLEM SOLVING

Sometimes the experience of depression can tell you something about problems in your life that need to be addressed. The question you want to ask yourself is, "What is contributing to my feeling, thinking, and acting in a depressed way?" Problem areas may not have caused your depression, but they may be significant sources of stress. Do any of these typical stressors apply to you?

- school performance issues
- problems with friends
- problems with other kids who aren't friends
- family difficulties
- problems with a teacher, coach, or other adult
- a loss in your life
- illness
- a recent life change (like moving or changing schools)

In some cases, problems can be solved, managed, or at least improved. You may be able to make changes that help, or you may be able to get assistance that makes a difference. If you're having trouble with school, a job, or a sport, you may need to work on developing specific skills.

In other cases, you cannot change the situation, so you need skills for dealing with stressors more effectively. Some problems may not be directly solvable, so you will want to seek avenues for coping with difficulties.

CONSIDER THIS: *Recognize the limits of your control.*

Take control of the things you can.

Once you have identified your current areas of stress, consider whether these are solvable problems or whether these are situations that can't change. For example, there are concrete steps a person can take if they are worried about a grade on a test. But if your family recently moved to a new town, you can't move back. In that case, you need to learn to cope with the move. You'll read more about coping with situations you can't change in the next chapter.

THINKING STRATEGICALLY ABOUT CHANGE

1. Make a chart of current difficulties you face. Put a "C" next to those you can *change* on your own. Put an "H" next to the ones for which you need *help*. Put an "A" next to those that can't change and that you'll need to *accept*.

2. Where you've put a "C," make a note about how you can make a change. Where you've written "H," note who can help and how. Next to problems where you've written "A," write an idea of how you can accept that you must cope with the problem, and how you can keep that problem from interfering with other areas of your life.

3. In the final column, write down what is most likely to happen as a result of these actions. Record how your coping strategies might offset the discomfort from experiences or events that you cannot change.

STRATEGIES FOR SOLVABLE PROBLEMS

When you can directly address a troubling situation, there are problem-solving strategies you can use.

CREATE A PLAN OF ACTION

Step 1: Identify the problem.

Step 2: Figure out what you would like to see happen.

Step 3: Brainstorm several possible solutions.

Step 4: Evaluate each solution. Which ones are possible and likely to be effective?

Step 5: Choose a solution and try it.

Step 6: Assess the outcome. How well did your plan work? Do you need to create a second plan of action?

For example, let's say you frequently have difficulty understanding your math homework. If you decide you don't like to think about it, you might just not hand in the homework, and then become upset as your grade goes down. But you could try to address the problem directly and find a better solution.

CONSIDER THIS: *Everyone has problems.*

Adapting requires searching for solutions.

1. Write down the problem: "Sometimes I don't understand my math homework."
2. Write down what you would like to see happen: "I want to finish the homework and turn it in so I get credit."

3. Brainstorm possible solutions: "Call a friend, email the teacher, spend more time on the homework and try harder to get the answers, ask my dad for help."

4. Evaluate each possible solution: "I can call a friend sometimes, but I don't want to overdo it. My teacher did say we can email him, so I probably should. I really don't think spending more time on the homework will help. My dad and I usually end up arguing when he tries to help with homework."

5. Choose a solution and try it: You might decide to sometimes call a friend and sometimes email the teacher in order not to overdo asking for help from one person. Try that for two weeks and then evaluate whether or not it helped.

6. Note how well your plan worked: Is your strategy working? Do you need to brainstorm more possible solutions?

CONSIDER THIS: *In life there are no "right" answers.*

Problem solving requires flexibility and persistence.

ROADBLOCKS TO EFFECTIVE PROBLEM SOLVING

If your action plan doesn't work, it may be because you've run into one of several common roadblocks. Let's look at them in turn.

Defining the problem. The first type of roadblock can occur when you define the problem. The way you choose to describe a problem can profoundly impact how successful you will be at solving it. This is particularly true if you use descriptions based on the types of depressive thinking we talked about earlier. For instance, for the problem we just talked about, if you defined the problem as your being "dumb," it would be pretty hard to think of ways to change that.

When a problem seems unsolvable, it can help to "reframe" it. Reframing refers to taking a different perspective or defining something in a new way. If you've labeled your problem using depressive thoughts (such as "all or nothing" thinking, categorical thinking, or catastrophizing), the very description of the problem may block your view of possible solutions.

As you define a problem, consider several possible ways of looking at it. Ask yourself, "What is it I really want (or don't want)?" Often becoming aware of your depressive thoughts and challenging them can help to give you a new perspective on a problem. Then choose the description of the problem that seems to suggest solutions that could work.

Becoming overwhelmed. At times you may have great ideas about ways of solving a problem but be overcome with anxiety about making a change or fear that you'll fail. You might feel shy about asking for help that you need, or just lack the energy to follow through on your plan because of depression. Remember that breaking down a task into smaller, easier steps can help to make it easier to move forward. You don't need to start with a giant leap. Baby steps will still help you to progress.

Quitting too soon. You know that old saying "If at first you don't succeed, try, try, again"? Once you've thought of a reasonable solution and followed through on it, there's a chance it may not work. This doesn't mean that there's no solution. It may be that you're being impatient with yourself and need to try that solution for a longer period of time. Or it may be that it's time to go through the process of problem solving again. Ask yourself if there's a different way to look at the problem. If you're unable to get yourself to follow through on a plan, consider whether there is an even smaller step you can take to get started.

The hurdle of anger. Stressful situations can cause a range of emotions. One of the most difficult is anger, an emotion that can be amplified by depression. When you are angry, it can be difficult to think clearly or stay in control of your behavior. And that can make effective problem-solving challenging. At those times you may need to start by calming your anger. Dealing with upsetting incidents and sources of anger is a challenge for everyone. Anger comes in many flavors: frustration, irritability, fury, annoyance, and so forth. Some forms of anger are mild or fleeting. Others can be very intense.

SORTING OUT FEELINGS OF ANGER

List different words for anger on index cards, or type them into a document on your computer. Once you have at least 10, rank them in order of intensity. As situations arise, consult your rankings to help you put your feelings into words.

OVERCOMING THE HURDLE OF ANGER

Anger of different intensities requires different strategies to calm yourself. Typically, the more intense the anger, the more you feel it physically. You also may find that you feel anger in different parts of your body, depending upon how strong the anger is. For instance, if you are just momentarily annoyed (and maybe feeling it as tension in your head or a clenched jaw or a stomach ache), the best strategy might be to just tell yourself to "let it go." Moderate anger is often felt as rapid breathing, tightness in your throat, and agitation that makes you feel a need to move. If what you're experiencing is rage, though, you may feel as if your whole body is wound up. You might feel teary-eyed, your fists might be clenched, and you might have a sense of wanting to explode. When anger is intense, you will need to find a way to calm it down before you can think clearly about how to solve the problem that caused it or deal effectively with those you're mad at.

Cooling angry thoughts. You learned in the previous chapters about how your thoughts are connected to your feelings. Take a look at these thoughts. Which ones would make a person angrier and which would help cool the anger?

__"I can't stand that guy."
__"I'll never get this to work."
__"I can handle it."
__"The teacher always lets her get away with it."
__"This is a temporary annoyance and will pass if I ignore it."
__"I don't need to get worked up about this."

Through practice, you can train yourself to think in a way that helps cool you off. Then you will be in a better frame of mind to talk about what is making you angry and use respectful language to get your point across:

"I don't like that."
"I'm so frustrated because . . . "
"I am angry because . . . "
"I am hurt when you . . . "

When anger makes a problem worse. For some people, anger can erupt in ways that make frustrating situations worse or that even cause additional problems in other parts of life. Sometimes this happens when sadness over not being able to reach one's

SORTING OUT FEELINGS OF ANGER, PART II

Keep notes about experiences that made you feel angry. Record what happened, how intense your anger was (using the ranking scale you devised), what you said and did, and how it ended. You may find that as you are learning to differentiate between different levels of anger, you may be able to let go of the small annoyances more easily. On the other hand, if some things still bother you, you may want to think of ways to address the problem if you can. Is there anything you wish you had done differently? Is there anything you can do now about something that's still bothering you?

goals leads to angry defensiveness. Yep, in addition to anger leading to sadness, sometimes sadness can result in anger! Here's an example:

Brandon used to get along well with his parents, but lately they are getting on his nerves. He comes home from school and goes straight up to his room. His mother knocks on his door and he growls, "Come in." She asks him about his day. Brandon glares and says, "It was school. What do you expect?" His mother replies, "I don't like that attitude." And pretty soon both are yelling.

What happened? Brandon is acting irritable and angry, but what he isn't saying is how sad he is. He isn't saying it partly because he isn't aware of his own thoughts and can't understand his own emotions. In his confusion, he is taking it out on his mother.

Brandon's mother wisely waits for Brandon to calm down and then asks him if they can talk. She helps him identify his emotions. They talk about how he is sad about not making the varsity basketball team and how worried he is about his grades. Once they sort out his emotions, Brandon is able to recognize his angry response to his mother's innocent query. They agree that he needs some time to chill after school and that it's best if she waits to talk to him.

As you have seen, some thoughts fuel your anger and make it worse, and some decrease your anger. After talking it over with his mother, Brandon realized he was thinking "Mom is always in my face. She should back off." When his mother suggested that she reached out to him because she cares, he was able to change his thought: "Mom cares about me, but I'm wiped out when I first get home from school and I need a break." After identifying his emotions and thoughts, he and his mother were able to problem-solve and come up with a plan that worked for both of them.

CONSIDER THIS: *An erupting volcano will make all living things flee. Cool down and talk calmly in order to be heard.*

Assertiveness. Expressing strong or uncomfortable emotions doesn't have to involve going into a rant or losing control. In fact, expressing anger in that way will probably backfire and leave you in a worse position. Nonetheless, you need to be able to speak up for yourself. This is called being "assertive," and is a very important skill. Being assertive is very different from yelling or being aggressive. It means expressing yourself in a way that invites other people to respect your interests, concerns, and emotions. And it's better than keeping your emotions inside of you. When you don't speak up for yourself, other people can take advantage of you. Some people are worried that if they speak up, others won't like them. They think that it's wrong to be angry. But you have a right to your needs and emotions. Others won't know what you are thinking and feeling—unless you tell them.

ASSERTIVENESS

1. Say what's bothering you.

2. Say how you feel.

3. Ask for what you want.

4. Say how that change will make you feel.

Here's how Alicia practiced being assertive. She and her friend Tasha were shopping for prom dresses. Alicia spotted a beautiful shimmery blue gown that she was excited to try on. Tasha liked it as soon as she saw it draped across Alicia's arm. Tasha said, "Oh, I think that style will look better on me—I'll try it on first."

What should Alicia say? Follow the steps to being more assertive:

1. State what it is that's bothering you. Alicia could say, "Tasha, I'd like to try the blue dress first."
2. State how you feel. Alicia could say, "It makes me upset when you say that you will look better in this dress than I will."
3. Ask for what you want. Alicia could say, "I hope you will help me find a nice dress for prom."

4. State how you'll feel if others respect your needs. Alicia could say, "When we help each other out, it makes me so happy that you are my friend!"

Yelling or stomping off or refusing to do something you are asked to do is aggressive, not assertive. Aggressive talk or actions are hurtful and inappropriate and make things worse. Keeping quiet and just going along is passive. While it doesn't hurt others, it hurts you in the long run. People who keep their thoughts and feelings to themselves end up overwhelmed and likely to lash out when it's finally all too much.

PRACTICING ASSERTIVENESS

Think about a time when you wish you'd been more assertive. What do you wish you'd said or done? How do you think things might have turned out differently? Be careful not to criticize yourself about what happened. Use your past frustration to help you plan for changes in your behavior the next time a similar situation arises.

By practicing assertiveness, you won't be holding it all in, yet you'll be expressing yourself in a way that doesn't hurt others. Even if you state your wants and needs directly, you won't always get what you want, but you will sometimes. You'll command respect and improve your sense of self-worth in the process.

When you recognize and acknowledge to yourself what you are feeling, practice thoughts that reduce anger, and talk respectfully and calmly about problems, you are more likely to stay in control. When you address problems assertively and straightforwardly, you will likely find solutions that help you be less depressed.

EXPLOSIVE, PASSIVE, OR ASSERTIVE?

You don't understand the teacher's explanation of the lesson. You:

1. Throw a fit when you get home and yell about what a terrible teacher you have.

2. Do nothing and hope the information won't be on a future test.

3. Ask the teacher if you can meet with them because you need some extra help.

Kids you are hanging out with want to see a movie you don't want to see. You:

1. Get angry and stay home instead of going out.

2. Say nothing and just go along even though this eats up your entertainment budget for the week.

3. Say "I'm not really interested in that movie," and suggest an alternative.

Someone calls you stupid. You:

1. Scream at them and call them names back.

2. Say nothing or laugh it off.

3. Tell them in a calm voice that you're sorry if they're upset and that if they can calm down, you're willing to talk about it.

Your parents ask you to do the dishes. You:

1. Yell that they're always interrupting you to do this and that.

2. Do the dishes even though you are overwhelmed by needing to study for a test, work on a project, and soccer practice that took longer than usual today.

3. Explain that you're under a lot of pressure today and ask if you can skip the dishes tonight and help out more on the weekend.

If you mostly answered with 1s, you may have a short fuse and may actually find others more receptive to your needs if you try using an assertive approach. If you answered with 2s, you may be letting others infringe on your needs. If you tended to answer with 3s, you're doing a good job of speaking up for yourself.

Journal Idea

Consider times when you are angry or frustrated and either act in ways that make the situation worse or withdraw without getting your needs met. As you face these situations, record how you might act assertively in the future. How might that change the outcome you experienced?

In a Nutshell

1. Practice following the six steps of effective problem solving: identify the problem, figure out what you would like to see happen, brainstorm about possible solutions, evaluate solutions, choose a solution and try it, and assess the outcome.

2. Learn to identify these common roadblocks to problem solving: defining the problem in a way that doesn't lead to possible solutions, forgetting to start with manageable steps, quitting too soon, and letting anger get in the way of clear thinking, planning, and action.

3. Remember that assertiveness is a valuable skill that allows you to express what you want or need or stick up for yourself.

CHAPTER 7
ACTIVE COPING

When you have problems that can't be directly solved, you need to find ways to adjust. Some examples of these kinds of problems are parents divorcing, the death of a loved one or pet, injury or illness, moving to a new home and school, or a friendship ending. There's plenty we are not in control of in these kinds of situations. Yet there are many ways to handle difficulties in your life. Even when you can't directly change a situation, you have choices about what to do in response.

DEVELOPING A COPING PLAN

Just as when you apply a problem-solving approach, taking time to plan a coping strategy (rather than just giving in to being upset) is important. Try to generate as many options as you can for investing your time and energy in ways that help you get through tough times. If the challenge is an overwhelming one, you may want to consult a parent or a therapist for suggestions.

Some options might be to distract yourself with meaningful activities or to make new friends or to find people who can provide support. Brainstorm a variety of actions. Think about the pros and cons of each one. Then employ the one with the most pros and fewest cons. When you identify a problem and use a coping strategy, you are being *proactive*—you are focusing on what you can do in a tough situation to help yourself feel better. While you may still be upset, you are keeping an unsolvable problem from taking over and intruding on all aspects of your life.

> **CONSIDER THIS:** *Fretting over bad things you can't change robs you of energy.*
>
> *Choose to direct your efforts toward activities that will invigorate and sustain you.*

Once you've identified such a problem, you can limit the time and situations in which you attend to it, find ways to distract yourself from it, and focus energy and attention on more positive things in your life. Check out Keisha's response to a problem she could not solve directly. She had to consider her alternatives and choose the best one for her:

Keisha is entering her freshman year in high school. When she was in middle school, she got caught up in a conflict between two groups of friends and ended up left out. She feels betrayed by girls she has known since she was in first grade. She worries that high school will be more of the same, and also believes she has no support group as she makes this big transition. She spends the summer playing too many video games and avoiding places like the pool where she might see kids from school. She is really down in the dumps.

Finally, Keisha decides to do something different. She thinks about a number of options. She can get a volunteer job that is meaningful to her. She can try to get some babysitting jobs. She can take a pottery class. She can join an activity at her high school. Keisha evaluates her options. Since she is a pretty decent athlete, Keisha decides to sign up to play soccer. She's not so sure she wants to do it, but she goes to the pre-season practice. It feels good to be active. She meets some other girls who will be in her class and who don't know her old group. She's surprised at how eager everyone is to make new friends. By the time school starts, Keisha is happier. She has met a few girls she knows well enough to sit with at lunch and talk to between classes.

Someone looking in from the outside might think that Keisha just got over her hurt, but the improvement involved much more active choices. The changes Keisha made were not huge ones, but they were important.

1. Keisha identified one of her strengths (being a good athlete) and used it as a coping strategy (getting more exercise) and as a way to increase her social contacts (meeting teammates).
2. Keisha accepted that her middle-school group was caught up in conflicts she could do nothing about. She chose to back away for the time being and focus on developing alternative social supports.

Keisha couldn't change what happened with her middle-school friends, but she could consider actions that helped her handle a tough situation.

DEVELOPING COPING STRATEGIES THAT ARE RIGHT FOR YOU

Learning to handle your emotions at difficult points in your life will help you to think clearly and make good decisions for yourself. To manage your emotions, learn to develop a variety of coping strategies, ones that fit your personality, abilities, and interests.

When you get upset, it is *your* job to calm yourself down. Experiment with what works for you. Depending on the situation, you might choose to do something active, or to do something creative, or to chill out, or to connect with someone. It can help to have some ideas handy because it's hard to think when you're upset.

Create four lists that you write on paper, store on your phone, or put down on index cards. Title your lists "Move," "Make," "Chill," and "Connect." Give yourself room to add to your lists as you think of other ideas. Here are some sample lists:

MOVE

- Shoot some baskets.
- Jump rope.
- Take a walk.
- Turn on music and dance.
- Ride a bike.
- Lift weights.

MAKE

- Draw or paint.
- Knit, sew, or crochet.
- Make up new lyrics to a song you like.
- Write a poem.
- Cook (soups and salads offer easy opportunities for creativity).
- Build something.
- Rehab an old piece of furniture.

CHILL

- Read.
- Take a mini-nap.
- Go to a quiet spot and look at cloud formations.
- Look at the stars.
- Take a bath (add bubbles if you like them, or sing to your heart's content).
- Practice some relaxation exercises (see Chapter 8 for ideas).

CONNECT

- Call a friend just to talk.
- Come up with a plan for a fun activity with a friend or group of friends. Get in touch and suggest it. If no one is free, be sure to make a note and try your idea later.
- Sit with a parent. Ask about their day and tell them something about yours.
- Go to a place where you can be with others, even if you don't necessarily want to talk. Doing homework at the library is one such idea.
- Invite a sibling to play a game.
- Stay after school and chat with other kids.
- Go to a sporting event or science fair at school, even if you don't participate.
- Attend a local festival.
- Volunteer to read to younger kids at a daycare center.

Access your lists when you need a quick source of ideas for you to take action to feel better when you get down or upset. The lists can serve as reminders of actions you can take to help you cope with situations that you can't change. It's okay if there's overlap between the lists (for instance, gardening can include both movement and creativity). Some of the ideas may require some prior planning, and that's fine—keep what you need on hand for moments when you are upset, or so you can regularly engage in activities that help you cope every day. Add to your lists as often as necessary, and review them frequently to remind yourself of all the methods you have for active coping.

DEVELOPING YOUR OWN COPING GAME PLAN

When you are overwhelmed or upset it can be hard to come up with a plan to deal with difficult emotions the moment you need one. At those times it can be helpful to have some "go to" strategies to distract yourself ready and waiting. Consider taking a little time when you are pretty content or at peace to plan for the inevitable bumps along the way. Here are a few ideas:

1. Start to collect postcards with inspiring or comforting pictures. (In the meantime you can use index cards—if you are artistic you can decorate one side.) On each one write something positive about yourself. Keep them in a special place and add to them regularly.

2. Make a playlist of calming music.

3. Make a playlist of music you like to dance to.

4. Develop a list of "inspirational quotes" or biographies (or movies) of inspirational people. You can easily find some good ones on the Internet. Choose ones that seem helpful to you.

5. Be a careful observer of other people's coping language. Write down in your journal or on index cards what you hear people say or do that will likely help them cope.

As you develop your coping mechanisms, recognize what you can and cannot change, and invest some energy in positive actions, you will be better able to manage the roller coaster of emotions that are part of being a teenager. In the next few chapters, you will learn the importance of self-care, expanding your social life, and developing your strengths. When you learn and practice a repertoire of coping strategies, you will be better able to climb your way out if you find that you're starting to slip into a depressed hole.

Journal Idea

Use your journal to make some observations about what coping strategies work best for you. Do you respond well to being physically active? Do you tend to do better by engaging your brain or your creative side? Does it help you to reach out to other people? How easy or difficult is it for you to follow through on using your coping strategies, and what can you do to put them into action more easily in the future?

In a Nutshell

1. Having coping methods in the face of problems that can't be solved will give you important resources against depression.

2. Moving, making, chilling, and connecting are four types of coping strategies you can develop.

3. Develop a list of coping strategies that fit you—and use them when you need to! Developing a proactive plan for coping is an important safeguard against depression.

CHAPTER 8
THE MIND-BODY CONNECTION

As a teenager, you have lots of choices in your life: what music to listen to, what school clubs to join, what sports to play, what websites to check, and on and on. Amid all of these options are daily choices regarding self-care. Will you make choices that increase or decrease your stress? Will you make choices that protect your health and well-being or hurt you in the long run? Increasing your mind-body connection will help you to manage upsetting emotions, such as anger and frustration, and lessen depression. When you are calm and healthy, you are better able to control your emotions and face life's challenges.

Your mind and body are connected, and each has an impact on the other. You experience stress as thoughts and emotions and as physical sensations in your body. For example, when you make a presentation to a large group, you might worry about how it will go and you might feel tightness in your stomach. Or, when something sad happens, your whole body might feel tired. Because your mind and body work together, there are steps you can take that involve both to keep yourself emotionally healthy.

TAKE CARE OF YOURSELF

The mind-body connection begins with what you do to take care of yourself on a daily basis. Taking care of yourself may sound easy and obvious but it is neither. Yet it is essential. You need to have the energy to handle stress and difficulties. When you get enough rest, relaxation, exercise, and nutritious food, you are well prepared to meet life's challenges with resilience. Resilience is the ability to bounce back from negative events. A ball that's become deflated won't bounce very effectively if it meets the stress of being thrown on a floor, having lost its resiliency. It will recover, though, if it's filled with air. Just like that ball, you need to pump yourself up so you can bounce back from stressors in your life. You can strengthen your resilience by committing to taking care of yourself.

You need to figure out what works for you. You won't find a one-size-fits-all solution to lifestyle changes that will improve your outlook and help you cope, but there are some basics that are good for you to know.

CONSIDER THIS: *Even the smallest healthy change*

counts as a change toward greater health.

First things first: sleep. Many factors contribute to depression. Some, like genetics, are not easily controlled, but others are more so. One of these is sleep. Although we've already said that depression can cause changes in sleep, lack of sleep can also trigger depression. Not getting enough sleep can make it hard to think clearly and concentrate well. It can add to your vulnerability by interfering with healthy eating patterns. Lack of sleep can even make acne worse, and that won't help matters!

Getting enough sleep can be a real challenge when you have school, afterschool activities, maybe a job, and homework!

Did You Know? *Sleep and the teenage body*

Research has shown that when you hit your teens your biological clock changes. Your body, which was once ready to settle in for the night at 9 p.m., is now sending out signals that bedtime is at 11. At the same time, your body is still growing and changing, and requires 8 to 10 hours of sleep a night to function well.[1]

Getting enough sleep is difficult for many teens. If your sleep is getting away from you, beware . . . depression may start to take over.

How do you know if your sleep schedule is becoming unhealthy? Consider these questions:

- Is your sleep schedule steady or do you "binge sleep" on weekends? Binge sleeping is a possible sign of not getting enough sleep during the week. If you are participating in weekend sleepovers, you may not be getting enough sleep on the weekend either.
- Do you have trouble falling asleep? This could mean that your routine just before bedtime is too stimulating. You might need to turn off the electronics or stop chatting with friends a bit earlier.

[1] AAP supports childhood sleep guidelines. (2016, June 13). *Healthy Children*. Retrieved from https://www.healthychildren.org/English/news/Pages/AAP-Supports-Childhood-Sleep-Guidelines.aspx

TRACKING YOUR ZZZZZZZs

Create a chart like the one below to keep track of your sleep patterns: when you went to bed, when you got up, whether you slept through the night, whether you napped during the day. Also note whether you did okay the next day or felt too tired. Make a note of what your mood was like. You may have to keep this up for a while before you see patterns emerge. If it seems that your sleep is not what it could be, think about one change you could make to your sleep habits, and track the impact that change makes over a period of two weeks.

Date	Bedtime	Woke Up	Total Nap Time	Total Sleep Time	Comments
Jan. 5	10:00 p.m.	6:30 a.m.	0 min.	8 hrs. 30 min.	Rested, calm

If you are having a hard time waking up in the morning because you did not get enough sleep, you may have pushed back your internal time clock—your circadian rhythm. The master clock in your brain may be signaling you to a late bedtime and late wake-up time. If so, you need to make efforts to move to an earlier bedtime. Try moving your bedtime 15 minutes earlier. If you don't fall asleep in 30 minutes, get up and, if possible, go to another room to read, listen to music, or draw (no electronics or screen time). When you are sleepy, try coming back to bed. This way, you will associate

TEN WAYS TO IMPROVE YOUR SLEEP

- Go to bed at a regular time each night that allows you to get at least 8 hours of sleep.
- Try to keep your wakeup time regular as well.
- Keep the electronics out of the bedroom.
- Turn off all screens at least an hour before bed.
- Stop homework at least half an hour (and preferably an hour) before bed.
- Don't exercise within the hour before bedtime (though earlier exercise will help with sleep).
- Avoid large meals or lots of liquid at bedtime.
- Skip the afternoon and evening caffeine. (Be aware of hidden caffeine in chocolate and soft drinks.)
- Develop a relaxing routine just before bed. Good options include reading, writing in your journal, listening to soft music, or meditating.
- Avoid naps until you are falling asleep readily at bedtime.

your bed with sleep and not with any other activities. At first, you may not fall asleep any earlier, but if you keep up this practice, your body will adjust to an earlier bedtime. This may take a couple of weeks and it requires a lot of patience, but it's worth it. If you have any other sources of interference with your sleep, such as snoring or leg cramps, see your physician for medical evaluation.

What should you do during the time you are in bed while you are waiting to fall asleep? Some relaxation techniques, described later in this chapter, may help.

Next up: exercise. Another way to take care of yourself is through physical activities. Exercise has been shown to help with depression.

If you play sports, you are already exercising, but if you don't, keep in mind that exercise does not have to be formal or hard. Ride your bike, take a walk, or swim. Exercise is helpful because it causes the release of endorphins in the brain. (Endorphins are neurotransmitters that improve our moods.) It takes your mind off your troubles, keeps you healthy, and gives you a break from stressful tasks. And, most important, it lessens depression.

WINTER WALKING

Taking a midday walk may offer double the value in the winter: a bit of mild exercise and exposure to sunlight to combat the effects of less daylight. (See Chapter 1 for more information about seasonal variations in mood.)

Nutrition and your health. Researchers have shown that good nutrition protects against depression. When you are busy, it can be hard to establish healthy eating patterns. But when you fuel your body with nutritious food, you have the energy to get through the day and be more alert. You may already know these important tips, but they are worth repeating:

- Don't skip breakfast. Eat regular meals so you won't crave junk food.
- Eat a variety of foods, including fruits and vegetables, proteins, and whole grains. Drink water.
- Cut back on unhealthy fats and sugary foods. Have some healthy snacks in addition to occasional treats. Skip the soft drinks.

Ideas for healthy snacks:

- Celery and peanut butter
- A bowl of oatmeal
- Low-fat or fat-free yogurt with fruit
- A handful of walnuts
- Fruit
- Air-popped popcorn

TAKE A NIBBLE AT HEALTHIER EATING

Changing eating habits can be hard, and a plan to eat nothing but healthy food all the time is bound to fail. Instead consider starting with one small change in your eating habits. For example:

- Exchange the crunch of chips for the crunch of a vegetable.
- Sip on a healthy breakfast smoothie instead of gobbling sugary cereal.
- Push aside that soft drink and sip on a low-sugar iced tea instead.
- Slather your whole grain bread with peanut butter and skip the butter, jelly, or chocolate spread.
- Grab a hard-boiled egg after school in place of cookies.

Avoid cigarettes, alcohol, and drugs. Good health also depends on avoiding harmful substances like tobacco, alcohol, and drugs.

When people are depressed, they sometimes turn to such substances in an attempt to block out the feelings and thoughts that make them sad or angry. But tobacco is dangerous and a known cause of lung cancer. Alcohol is actually a depressant and it won't help with low mood. It also can result in dependence or problem behaviors that can create added difficulties in one's life. Even if

103

Evidence indicates that it may be smoking that comes before the depression, suggesting that smoking may actually increase the likelihood of depression.[2]

marijuana is legal where you live, it is ill-advised for teenagers whose brains are still growing and will continue to do so well beyond age 20. Marijuana use can decrease judgment and interfere with learning, memory, and coordination. It can also lead to depression. In fact, in teens who use marijuana to deal with thoughts of depression, it may make symptoms worse or even trigger more serious mental illness.[3] Check out http://teens.drugabuse.gov/ for more details.

When you take care of your body through getting plenty of sleep, engaging in exercise, and eating healthily, your efforts will directly affect your sense of well-being. A healthy mind-body connection requires a healthy body! But adopting and maintaining healthy habits may not be enough. Relaxation is also important to manage stress.

Relaxation. The goal of relaxation is to calm your body and your mind to reduce stress and tension and tame your emotions.

[2] Steuber, T. L. & Danner, F. (2006). Adolescent smoking and depression: Which comes first? *Addictive Behaviors*, *31*(1), 133–6.
[3] Meier, M. H., Caspi, A., Ambler, A., Harrington, H., Houts, R., Keefe, R. S. E., . . . Moffitt, T. E. (2012). Persistent cannabis users show neuropsychological decline from childhood to midlife. *Proceedings of the National Academy of Sciences 109*, No. 40, E2657–E2664.

HOW'S YOUR HEALTH REPORT CARD?

BEHAVIOR	GRADE E=Excellent! S=Satisfactory N=Needs Improvement	SUGGESTIONS FOR THE FUTURE
Sleep		
Exercise		
Nutrition		
Toxic Substances		

There are several methods that may help you achieve relaxation, such as guided imagery, deep breathing, meditation, and progressive muscle relaxation. A little about each:

Guided imagery is the use of visualization techniques to fill your mind with pleasing images. There are apps available that direct you through storytelling or descriptions. You can also find some on YouTube. Or you can write your own guided-imagery script and record it or memorize it. For example:

Close your eyes and picture a path in the woods. Follow the path up a steep hill. There's a quiet stream on your right. You can hear it rushing over stones. You can also hear the crunch of leaves under your feet. Let yourself "be" there. You have time to notice it all. The sun is shining down through the branches, and you feel its warmth on your face as you move through the patches of brightness. Near the top of the hill is a large tree. You decide to take a rest under it. As you look up through the branches, you think about the tree's experience of life. Even when you leave, this tree will remain. It will be here when you return. It will stand here quietly when it rains. It will be steady but transformed when it snows. It will change color in the fall and sprout leaves in the spring. But through all of these changes in the world, the tree will remain the same tree. And it will always exist in your mind's eye and be there when you need to rest against it.

WRITE YOUR OWN GUIDED-IMAGERY SCRIPT

1. Choose a favorite peaceful place, such as the beach or a mountain setting.

2. Use as many senses as possible to describe the details of your favorite place. What are the sights and smells and sounds?

3. Describe yourself experiencing this place in ways that are meaningful to you.

Deep breathing exercises can help you relax, calm your body, and let unhelpful brain chatter drift into the background.

Here is one example:

> Focus on your breath with long, easy inhales and exhales. Close your eyes and try counting slowly to seven with each inhale and to eight with each exhale. Exhale all your breath so you feel your lungs fully empty each time. If you become distracted by noises or your own thoughts, remind yourself that you don't need to engage with them. If you lose your breathing count that's okay: just start again counting in for seven and out for eight. Repeat at least three to five times.

And here is another:

> Lie on your back with your knees bent. Place one hand on your belly and the other on your chest. As you breathe in, imagine you are filling a balloon in your belly. Your hand will rise as your belly fills with air. The hand on your chest should not rise as much. As you exhale, just let your "balloon" slowly deflate. Allow yourself to feel more and more relaxed with each balloon breath.

And a third with some visualization thrown in:

> Close your eyes and imagine that the breath you take in is red while what you breathe out is blue. Visualize how the breath enters your nose, throat, and lungs and how the used air exits the same way. Notice how the air forms wisps, eddies, and clouds as it travels and how it is constantly changing.

Meditation is establishing a quiet internal state and a quiet mind by focusing attention away from unwanted thoughts and real-life worries. Meditation requires a quiet, calm place but only about 10 or 15 minutes of your time and something to focus on. Some popular choices to meditate on are:

- Words or sounds: Try repeating a simple sound such as "om." Start with an "ah" sound. Then gradually form an "o" shape with your lips and next move your lips to close. Notice how the sound changes and starts to move inward. This can be combined with deep breathing as you say (or think) "om" over a seven-count exhale.
- Positive statements to yourself: Choose ones that are believable to you. For example, you might repeat "At the center of my being, I am strong, I am calm, and I am safe" aloud three times slowly.
- Objects: Try staring at a candle flame or crackling fire. Just be careful that the flame is in a safe spot with nothing flammable around it. Stare into the flame and let it take you deep inside yourself.
- Walking: You might like to try walking meditation. Find a safe and comfortable place to walk outside. Start with some deep breaths to get in touch with the sensations in your body. Begin a normal pace focusing on your internal experience. If your attention drifts to sights or thoughts, just refocus to the details of how your body feels while walking. Notice your feet and how they feel, the left-right rhythm of your legs, and the swinging motion of your arms. As you scan your body, let go of tension, maintaining a steady inhalation and a steady exhalation. The key is to keep your focus on the sensations in your body.

CONSIDER THIS: *Many people think boredom is a cue to find something to do.*

Embrace unstructured moments as times to reflect, observe, and decompress.

Progressive muscle relaxation is a technique that helps you to relax by systematically helping muscles to let go of tension.

Tighten and relax each muscle group to let go of tension. Start with the top of your head and move gradually downward. Or begin at your toes or fingers and move toward the center of your body. Remember to include the muscles in your face. Work slowly through each muscle group. Hold the muscles tight for several seconds before you relax that body part. Notice how the release of tension feels.

Hypnosis typically incorporates several relaxation methods, but other techniques may also be employed. You can learn self-hypnosis through a therapist trained in this practice, or you can try a guided hypnosis app.

Active relaxation refers to techniques that involve movement as a means to relax. While the relaxation techniques previously described work well, especially at night in bed, sometimes a more active, directed type of relaxation during the day is also helpful. You might consider taking a yoga class or trying tai chi to help you focus and relax.

Specific methods of relaxation can be helpful additions to your day. You can take a break in other ways too. What do you enjoy? Unwind by drawing, reading for pleasure, doing a craft, listening to music, or playing a game. When you engage in activities you enjoy, you are finding balance in your life. You can better manage your many responsibilities and pressures when you give yourself time each day to do something relaxing.

Your body's health and well-being has a big impact on your emotions. Caring for your physical needs by eating well, exercising, getting enough sleep, and learning strategies to decompress from stress will help you care for your emotional health. If you've been neglecting yourself, now is a good time to make a commitment to give yourself the care you deserve!

Journal Idea

Try a method of relaxation three times and note your response. Try another one or two methods. Choose the one that was the most helpful to you and try it daily for a few weeks. Keep a record of your practice.

In a Nutshell

1. Caring for your body by getting adequate sleep, regular exercise, eating in healthy ways, and avoiding alcohol, drugs, and smoking have all been shown to help with depression.

2. There are many relaxation techniques that you can use to calm yourself, including guided imagery, deep breathing, meditation, and progressive muscle relaxation.

3. Active relaxation refers to techniques that involve movement as a means to relax. This includes activities like yoga and tai chi.

CHAPTER 9
DEVELOPING YOUR STRENGTHS

It's not surprising that people tend to focus on their weaknesses. When we make New Year's resolutions, we usually pick an area to improve. While there's nothing wrong with that, it may be even more important to take stock of your strengths. When you are depressed, you are likely to focus too much on what you don't do well and on your problems and overlook what you are good at and the positive things in your life. You may easily be able to turn on a recording in your head that ticks off the negatives but be at a loss when asked "What are you good at?"

TAKE STOCK OF YOUR STRENGTHS

If this sounds at all like you, you may need to work on building a more balanced (and *accurate*) inner recording by taking stock of your strengths. Keep in mind that the focus here is not on identifying where you are perfect but on helping you to acknowledge the parts of yourself that you can appreciate and enjoy. Here are a few ideas to get you started. Challenge yourself to identify at least five strengths from the categories below.

What skills do you have? This is probably what you think of first when others ask you what you're good at. If you struggle with depression, you may immediately turn the question around and start thinking about what you're NOT good at. But resist this automatic reaction. Really take some time to think about what skills you have:

- What do you do well in school? Be specific. Don't just list subjects like English or biology or academic skills like reading or writing (though of course they all count) but also more general abilities like memorizing information or doing projects, making mental connections, having curiosity, or thinking outside the box.
- What hobbies, activities, and other fun things do you engage in? What skills do you demonstrate when doing them? Again, be very specific. If you play a sport, what is your best skill? In addition to abilities like fast running, include skills such as staying alert to what's happening. Do you play an instrument, write song lyrics, or sing well (even if it's only in the shower)? Do you have a good sense of rhythm or musical sensitivity? If you like to put outfits together, do you have a good sense of color or proportion?

> **CONSIDER THIS:** *Telling others what you do better than they do is bragging.*
>
> *Telling yourself what you do well is having confidence.*

What personal and emotional strengths do you have? Here the focus is on what kind of a person you are, including traits you were born with or personal qualities you have developed over time. The emphasis is not on whether or not you are the best at these specific skills but rather on whether you can identify and draw upon them when you need to.

- What are your native gifts? Are you smart? Are there areas where you have talent? Are you creative? Are you athletic? Are you self-aware? Insightful?
- What abilities do you possess that help you to deal with demands and stresses? Do you exhibit self-control when it's called for? Do you have common sense and good judgment ("street smarts")? Can you keep things in perspective when a problem arises? Are you a good problem-solver? Are you industrious? Can you laugh at yourself?
- What aspects of self-discipline do you demonstrate? If you play a musical instrument, that is certainly a skill, but you may also demonstrate self-discipline when you practice. Are you an effective planner? Are you organized? Do you manage your time effectively? Do you follow through? Can you identify activities that were hard at first but that you kept working at (in other words, do you have "stick-to-itiveness")?

What people skills do you have? Being sensitive to and tolerant of others is an important ability that impacts many aspects of your life. Getting along with others is also very complicated, and no one is good at it all the time. Take some time to think about what you do when you are most satisfied with your interactions with others.

- How do other people experience you? Are you friendly? Are you fun to be with? Do you have a good sense of humor? Are you sensitive and caring? Are you thoughtful and kind? Are you generous with your time? Are you reliable?
- How do interactions with others go? Can you debate about differing opinions while remaining respectful? Do you speak up for yourself? Do you pay close attention to others when they speak? Do you tolerate other peoples' weaknesses and differences?

- Are you involved with others (friends, family, and/or your community)? Do you spend time with young kids? With adults? With older people? Do you work well with others?

Do you have a personal compass? When confronted with life choices, challenges, and problems, it can help to have a clear sense of what's important to you. Your values can give you confidence in the face of pressure from outside yourself, and guide you toward creating a life that's meaningful.

- Do you have a clear sense of what your personal values are? Is spirituality important to you? Are you religious? Do you make choices that reflect your values? Do you have a personal moral compass that guides your decisions? Do you know what aspects of life are most meaningful to you? Do you spend time reflecting on the gifts and talents that you have?

CONSIDER THIS: *A good sailor has a map, a compass, and a destination in mind.*

Evaluate what matters most to you to avoid being blown off course by the trivial.

Do you appreciate beauty? Being able to recognize and attend to parts of your environment that give you pleasure because of their aesthetic value is a special kind of strength. In the busy world of many distractions and pressures, the importance of being able to simply enjoy beauty for its own sake is easily overlooked. Take time to think about what you find special and moving in your life.

- Do you appreciate beauty? Do you like being out in nature? Do you enjoy music? Do you appreciate art? Is being creative a joyful experience for you? Do enjoy designing things? Do you appreciate a well-turned phrase or a clever pun? Do lyrics to songs impact you in a pleasurable way? Do you love good food?

MY PERSONAL STRENGTHS

Taking time to write down a list of your personal strengths is a valuable step toward acknowledging them.

My skills and areas of competence: _____

_____

My personal and emotional skills: _____

_____

My interpersonal skills: _____

_____

Values I keep in mind and live by: _____

_____

My artistic tastes and aesthetic sense of beauty: _____

_____

Other strengths I could focus more upon: _____

_____

Watch your language. As you think about your personal strengths and weaknesses, consider whether you tend to take a negative point of view about yourself. Notice the language you use when thinking about your pluses and minuses. Often, what you see as a weakness has another side that reflects strength. For instance, it's common for kids who are quiet and slow to make friends to label this as a weakness (poor conversationalist, not fun) when it may actually reflect a strength (good listener, thoughtful, considerate, reserved).

Critical labels you give yourself may also be more extreme than is true. Do you tell yourself that you're not a good student because you're not in the most challenging classes or getting the highest grades? Have you considered how far you've progressed in your coursework or how much your grade has improved? See if there are ways of recasting your language.

RETHINK YOUR "NEGATIVE" CHARACTERISTICS

Take one of your personal attributes that tends to bother you. Challenge yourself to consider whether that part of yourself has a positive side or allows you another area of strength. Or is that trait less completely true about you than you sometimes think? Can you think of times when you displayed its opposite? An example follows each question below:

- What is the attribute that bothers you?
  I have trouble accepting criticism.
- What bothers you about it?
  I get uncomfortable and think that I'm inadequate.
- Is there anything that co-exists with that part of yourself that you do like?
  I do like that I care about doing well.
- Would you lose anything if that aspect of yourself disappeared completely?
  I guess if I didn't mind criticism at all it might mean I wouldn't put as much effort in because I wouldn't care what others thought.
- Are there times when you don't act or think that way?
  When the criticism is really helpful, I don't mind it so much.

Paying attention to the good stuff is a strength. "Negative selective attention" can both contribute to depression and result from it. No one can pay attention to everything around them at all times.

Without being fully aware of it, we make lots of choices about what to attend to and what to ignore during any given day. If you give more attention to the negative things in life, it could lead to depression. At the same time, if you are depressed and unhappy about yourself or your life, you will tend to look for (selectively attend to) evidence that supports what you believe about yourself. Before you know it, you've jumped onto that loop of depression that we talked about in Chapter 3.

One way to refocus your attention on the positives in your life is to make a note each day of things that go well. They don't have to be huge things like winning an award or getting a date with the person you really like (though include those if they happen). The idea here is to help you to pay more attention to the ordinary good things in your day that you may be taking for granted. A list could include things like:

- I raised my hand and answered a question correctly in class.
- I did well at my music lesson.
- A kid I like smiled at me.
- The bush outside is flowering and it's so pretty.
- I saw the most hysterical video.
- We had my favorite dinner.
- The art project I'm working on is turning out to be cool.
- I like the book I'm reading for English.
- ____ asked my advice about ____.

Maybe a real-life example can help you understand how refocusing attention on the positive things in life can have a powerful impact:

Jackson believed that he was always letting people down. His grades in school were okay, but it seemed he could never quite get the grades everyone thought he should. He sometimes missed assignments, and then got overwhelmed when it came time to make them up in addition to his other work. He was a good athlete, but just didn't like practices and couldn't get into it. His parents always seemed to be on him about one thing or another, and he would snap at them and then feel guilty afterward. He often thought of himself as just a big loser.

Jackson's favorite teacher, the one he tended to confide in, suggested that he track small positive things that happened each day. He didn't think it could help, but it also didn't seem that hard, so he gave it a try. He began to show Mr. Sprag his list when they met for lunch every Wednesday. At first Mr. Sprag needed to prompt Jackson about what positive things he might include. After two weeks he was totally hooked. His list included lots of things he'd done to help out friends, his successes as an actor in skits in a theater class, compliments he'd gotten from his English teacher on his writing skills, his scouting activities, and his ability to solve computer glitches for his parents. After a few weeks of tracking the positive things in his life, Jackson was shocked at how differently he saw himself and how much more content he was.

CONSIDER THIS: *We write our own memoir each day.*

Choose to remember the things that reflect your strengths.

Get engaged. People who are more engaged tend to be happier. What does that mean? "Engagement" means being involved—not just doing things but being really into them. These are the things that you are passionate about, that you become lost in, or that you get satisfaction out of just for themselves (and not for what you may gain from them). Engagement can happen in activities or with other people. Being engaged can help you to be emotionally stronger. You can become more engaged by participating in new activities that hold a strong interest for you, putting more time or energy into activities that really matter to you that you already do, or simply interacting with energy and attention toward the people around you.

Being helpful to others can be an especially rewarding form of engagement—for them but also for you! Later in this book we'll talk about the fact that other people usually like it when you seek out their help. That works both ways. You can make big commitments to help others, like taking on a volunteer job or participating in charitable activities at your school or religious center. But you can also help others around you in small ways. You may find satisfaction in making a commitment each day to do one or more things to help others.

HOW DO YOU HELP?

What things do you do to help other people? How do you feel afterward? What would you like to add to that list?

As you track your efforts to reach out to others, don't forget the small stuff.

For example, your list might look something like this:

- Cleaned out the front closet—was happy when Mom and Dad saw I'd done it without even being asked. Liked it when Mom said this would give her a chance to just sit for a minute.
- Talked to the shy new kid at school—she's actually kind of sweet and seemed so glad to have someone reach out. Pumped me up!
- Told my sister I liked her hair—after she got over the shock, she seemed really happy. I was glad.

Helping others can feel awesome, but being engaged means more than that. It means doing what matters to you. When you get involved with activities that are important to you, you'll start to build skills and a sense of accomplishment. Your activities can be social (like being on a sports team or doing a play) or they can be things you do alone (like writing poetry, painting, or building things) or they may be something in between (like cooking). The more you participate in an activity about which you are passionate, the more it will become a part of you and the more satisfying it will be. Gaining a sense of competency can add to your list of things you are happy about and make you more resilient in the face of challenges.

Give yourself important feedback. You may find it easier to identify the strengths of others than to identify your own good qualities. Or you may only acknowledge your strengths briefly, moving on rapidly to focus on life's demands. Now that you've spent some time thinking about what your positive attributes are, put some time and energy into reminding yourself of them in a strong and emphatic way. This next exercise will probably seem a little strange the first few times you do it. That's okay. Try it anyway—no one else needs to know about it.

TELL IT LIKE IT IS

Stand in front of a mirror. Look yourself in the eye. Address your image as if you are talking to another person by saying "you" or using your name. Tell your mirror image four or five things that are true strengths or positive qualities that you possess. Try doing this once a day for a week. Does this make you more aware of what you like about yourself? Are you becoming more confident that these positive qualities are accurate descriptions of you? Are you able to gain a greater sense of appreciation for how important they are? [1]

[1] Starchesky, L. (2014, October 7). Why saying is believing: The science of self-talk. *NPR*. Retrieved from http://www.npr.org/blogs/health/2014/10/07/353292408/why-saying-is-believing-the-science-of-self-talk

The importance of resilience. All this focus on being more aware of your strengths can help you to become more able to deal with stress and, well, life! By being more aware of your strengths and building on them, focusing on the positives, and engaging with people and activities that you have a passion for, you will increase your resilience. Remember, resilience is the ability to bounce back when you get knocked down. The more resilient you are, the better able you will be to cope with life's problems, be flexible in the face of adversity, keep going when you become discouraged, and let go of disappointments.

The loop of depression spins in a negative direction, causing you to spiral downward. Part of getting that loop to spiral upward is to change your inner dialogue about yourself. Celebrating your own strengths and skills, clarifying who you are and what's important to you, and recognizing your positive impact will help fight depression, or prevent it from taking hold.

Journal Idea

This one sounds simple, but—we promise—it's crazy powerful! Make a note of four things that went well during the day. Don't limit yourself to big events. Part of the goal here is to make sure you're paying attention to the small and everyday things that are going well in your life as well as the bigger and more obvious ones.

In a Nutshell

1. If you are prone to depression, it is likely that you tend to pay too much attention to what you dislike about yourself and too little attention to what you're good at. By becoming aware of your strengths, however, you will have identified the resources you possess that will enable you to get through challenges.

2. It's important to have a sense of the things you value most, the things you see as important to both present and long-term goals. These core values serve as a personal compass to guide you on your way to being the kind of person you want to be.

3. Engagement means being actively involved: with activities, with other people, and with your world. People who are engaged tend to suffer less from depression.

4. Being aware of your own abilities and resources can help you to be more resilient when faced with challenges.

CHAPTER 10
STRENGTH IN NUMBERS

In addition to your personal strengths, your relationships with others will help you get through tough times. The people in your life can offer support by listening, helping you, offering you guidance, celebrating your successes, and reminding you of how terrific you are.

Friends and family have a big influence over how you think, feel, and behave. And, by the way, when we refer to friends, we do not mean the Facebook kind. We mean true friends with whom you share time together, people you talk with regularly. Other teens, family, and trusted adults can play a central role in how you see yourself, how you think about your life, and how you handle bumps in the road.

But when you are depressed, you may become withdrawn. You may actually avoid the very people who could help to pull you out of your withdrawal. Try spending some time thinking about your social supports, and practice reaching out to them in small ways. First, think about whom you can trust to have your back when things go wrong. The list may include parents, friends, siblings, teachers, coaches, a scoutmaster, neighbors, or a religious leader.

IDENTIFYING PEOPLE WHO HAVE YOUR BACK

Go ahead and make an actual written list of people who have your back when things aren't going well.

Okay, now write a list of the kinds of problems that have triggered depressed thoughts, feelings, or behaviors in the past. Everyone's list will be different, but a typical list could include:

- A fight with a friend
- Parents saying you can't do something
- Not doing well at something
- Disliking what you see in the mirror
- Being left out
- A romantic break-up
- Family problems

Now, next to each type of problem, write the names of the people on your support list who might be able to help in the particular situation. Try not to think about whether you'd be comfortable asking for that help. We'll get there in a moment.

For example:

A fight with a friend—Dad. (He will understand where I'm coming from and help me put this in perspective.)

My parents' fights freak me out—Sarah. (She knows I get stressed out about this. I can trust her to talk with me about how it affects me.)

Look at your lists. Do you think your social support list is too short? That might be an important clue that you should spend more time building relationships. Is it hard to think of which people on your social support list could help with a given problem? That could be a sign that you need to think more broadly about the kinds of people who might be important in your life, but it may also mean that you don't know how to reach out for support or that you've been reluctant to do so.

REACHING OUT FOR SUPPORT

If you think you need to develop the skill of seeking support from others, the first really important thing to keep in mind is that most people really like helping other people. Helping others makes a person feel trusted, competent, and like they're doing something valuable. That's true not just for other teens but for people of all ages. In addition, when one person helps another, it usually brings them closer emotionally. So seeking support can, in itself, help to build stronger relationships.

Even knowing that, it can be hard to tell someone else that you're down or that you have a problem. If you're not used to asking for support, take small steps at first. Some people can be helpful just by being with you. A friend might offer distraction from your ruminations or just some pleasant fun. An adult may give you some feedback that reminds you of things you have going for you.

To take it further, you can tell someone what you're upset about (without fully divulging how much it hurts). But don't just joke about it. If you do, you may get a joke back and that may hurt more. For example, if you feel overwhelmed and left out in big groups, you might try saying, "I'm thinking of skipping the dance because of all the cliques." See if that leads to a friend sharing their own experience of being left out, or to a teacher giving you hints about how to break into a group, or to a parent reminding you of what other kids like about you.

Once you have some experience with these small instances of receiving support, you might go further and start to share how much the stuff that bothers you *really* bothers you. If you're like most kids, you may be surprised by how much it helps just to tell other people that you are depressed. They may not be able to fix it, but it can help to know that they're there for you.

Increasing your social connections. It's pretty common for depression to be triggered by difficulties with friends. Sometimes the cause can be a problem with a current group of friends, but challenges with making new friends can also trigger depression. To make matters worse, when you are depressed, it often shows in your facial expressions, your posture, and even in how you dress, which may be a turnoff to the very kids you'd like to get to know. If you are often lonely, you can take some steps to make new or deeper connections to other teens.

> **CONSIDER THIS:** *Taking care of your friendships*
> *is one way of caring for yourself.*
>
> *Reach out to someone who matters to you.*

Making friends. The art of making friends isn't easy or straightforward. Below are a few tips we hope you'll find useful:

- It's easiest to make friends with people who share a common interest.

Obvious, maybe, but beware of chastising yourself for not being in with the popular crowd if you don't like doing the things they do. If what you love is cooking or reading, consider taking a cooking class or joining (or starting) a book club. If you don't have a special interest, joining a club or activity may help you develop one and meet people who also are learning something new.

- **Making friends requires being friendly.**

This doesn't mean that you need to become super outgoing if that's not your style, but you will need to talk to people and share your thoughts, experiences, and interests. You'll need to look welcoming (smile) and take the first step sometimes.

- **Making friends means taking risks.**

In order to make the move from acquaintances to friends, you can't always wait for the other person to move the friendship forward. So you may have to make an invitation to get together. If you tend to be shy or if you have a history of problems with friends, this can be scary. It's often easiest to ask the other person to do an activity that takes the pressure off having to find things to talk about. Watching a movie or playing paintball are examples that could work. And—very important—if someone turns down your invitation because they're busy, they just might be! Don't take this as a sign that they don't want to be friends. Try again!

- **Making friends requires being sensitive to others' emotions.**

Remember that you are not the only one in your school or neighborhood who is lonely or wants more friends. Be aware of other kids who might be really happy to have someone reach out to them. Be careful that your hesitancy about making an overture doesn't come across as just going through the motions. Remember that other people also may be insecure and need encouragement.

CONSIDER THIS: *Building a strong network of friends takes time and effort.*

Be the kind of friend you want others to be for you.

Keeping Friends. While making new friends during your teen years is important, you also want to put energy into keeping the friends you already have. If you are prone to depression, you may find that there are times when you withdraw from friends. Or your emotions may lead you to act in ways that may be misunderstood by those who are closest to you. If you think this is true about you, consider taking corrective action.

- If you've been withdrawn or unavailable, try suggesting a get-together or give special attention to a friend you think you may have accidentally neglected.
- If you've been short-tempered or unfair, apologize.

Dating. On top of all the other sources of stress—school, sports, homework, and so forth—dating can bring excitement but also another kind of pressure. Even if you are not yet dating, relationships with a love interest can take center stage, affecting your mood and your frame of mind. And if you really don't think you are ready to date, you may have to contend with direct and indirect challenges to that decision.

At times when your self-esteem is low, attention from a love interest can really perk you up. At the same time, you may not be as confident as you normally might be when someone is not being respectful of you, your emotions, or your needs outside of the relationship (like spending time with other friends).

IS YOUR RELATIONSHIP SUPPORTING YOUR POSITIVE OUTLOOK?

After time spent with your significant other, do you:

1. Wonder what they could possibly like about you?

2. Think the two of you have a lot in common?

3. Believe they see positive things about you that others miss?

When you've had a rotten day, does your special someone:

1. Tell you all the things you did that made things go wrong?

2. Reassure you that tomorrow is another day and a fresh start?

3. Point out the positive things you have going for you?

If you told your special someone that you wanted to spend the weekend with your friends, would they:

1. Get mad?

2. Tell you they'll be sad but that they'll get over it?

3. Let you know how much they like that you're such a good friend?

If someone else was flirting with your significant other, would they:

1. Flirt back?

2. Laugh it off?

3. Make it clear through words or actions that you are a couple?

(continued)

IS YOUR RELATIONSHIP SUPPORTING YOUR POSITIVE OUTLOOK? *(continued)*

When you say negative things about yourself, does your special someone:

1. Agree with you?

2. Brush it off?

3. Acknowledge that you're not perfect but that your pluses far outweigh your imperfections?

If you told your special person that you weren't ready to move things ahead sexually, would they:

1. Threaten to end the relationship (or hint that they might)?

2. Express a bit of frustration but accept your position?

3. Let you know that it doesn't change where the relationship stands?

If you mostly answered with 3s, lucky you! You seem to be in a relationship that provides support and a good sounding board. If you mostly answered with 1s, it may be that your "significant other" isn't up to giving you the kind of loving care you deserve.

Sex. Engaging in risky sexual activity is sometimes a symptom of depression. If you are sexually active, it can be tempting to use sex to try to lift yourself up when you're down. Be careful that you don't throw caution to the wind and take chances with unprotected sex, have sex with someone with whom you don't feel connected, or forget the impact that a sexual experience may have on another person. Don't let a short escape from depression create even bigger problems later.

Breaking up is so very hard to do. Remember that you are at a stage of learning about being in relationships. That means it's unlikely that a boyfriend or girlfriend you have right now is "the one." That means teens often have to deal with break-ups. And it's not just romantic relationships that can change. Having a falling out with a friend can be just as hard to cope with.

When you are depressed, it can be harder to bounce back from a relationship that ends. This may be a time when you are especially vulnerable and overwhelmed by self-criticism and distorted thinking. Turning to friends or to a trusted adult can help you keep perspective on what happened and on what it means to you as you move forward.

Being LGBTQ. Although in many areas of our society same-sex relationships are more accepted than at any time in the past, if you are LGBTQ (lesbian, gay, bisexual, transgender, queer, or questioning), you may encounter hurtful attitudes. If you are unsure about your sexual orientation or identity, you may experience pressure to define yourself before you are ready. If this happens, please identify and reach out to peers and adults you can trust for support.

HELP IS OUT THERE!

LGBTQ YOUTH ARE AT GREATER RISK FOR DEPRESSION THAN ARE THEIR HETEROSEXUAL PEERS

This is not because of their sexuality or identity but because of negative experiences such as discrimination and victimization.

If you are LGBTQ or are questioning your sexuality, you deserve to be treated with the same respect as everyone else. In addition to trusted adults in your family and community, check out this online resource: Sexual Minority Youth Assistance League (SMYAL) at www.smyal.org

Developing a network of people, including peers and adults, who can help you is good protection for navigating life's ups and downs. At the same time, helping others when they are having a rough time can give you an emotional boost too. Make sure there is reciprocity in your relationships—a give-and-take. Be there for others and let them be there for you.

HELP IS OUT THERE!

INTERPERSONAL PSYCHOTHERAPY FOR ADOLESCENTS

If you try our suggestions for expanding your social connections and you are not as successful as you'd like, you might be a good candidate for interpersonal psychotherapy for adolescents (IPT-A).

IPT-A is a brief therapy that is showing good results for depressed teenagers. It is increasingly available. Check this website to find therapist trained in IPT: https://iptinstitute.com/

Losing a friend or group of friends. A common but difficult challenge during your teen years can be losing a close friend or being dropped from a group of friends. Sometimes losing a friend can happen when someone moves or changes schools. At other times, though, friends can drift apart because of changes in interests and activities. And, often most painfully, long-term friendships can end over conflict or deeply hurt feelings. If this has happened to you and you want to resume the relationship, you may try to reach out to the other person and see if a disagreement can be resolved, an apology can put the friendship back on track, or other problem-solving strategies can restore your friendship.

Sadly, though, everyone loses friends over their lifetime. Trying too hard to hold onto a dying friendship or focusing on prior losses can make it harder to establish new friendships. Facing the fact that some such experiences of loss are part of life (though a painful part) can be the first step in letting go of the hurt, moving on, and allowing yourself to become open to others. Be especially careful about the story you tell yourself about this loss.

If you engage in negative distortions about the failed relationship and how and why it ended, you may be creating a false negative memory that can form a problematic script for subsequent friendships. For example, if a best friend starts to spend more time with other people, you could accept that the two of you no longer share the same interests you had when you were younger. If, on the other hand, you assume this loss means that you can't trust the people who are close to you, you may act mistrustful and find it difficult to make close friends in the future.

What to do about a depressed friend. Sometimes teens have concerns about dealing not with their own depression but with that of a friend. Remember that 5 percent of teens experience serious depression at some time. That means that, whether you're aware of it or not, you likely know someone else who is depressed. If a friend confides that they are experiencing difficulties and you are concerned, you might want to ask if they think they may need professional help. It can be a hard question to ask, but if they do need help, your bringing it up may be just what they need to take important steps to tackle their depression. If they say yes, help them think through which adults they are comfortable confiding in. Encourage them to do so, and ask if they'd like you to go with them for moral support.

HELP IS OUT THERE!

SEEKING HELP WHEN FRIENDS ARE CONSIDERING SUICIDE

Although it's important to keep a friend's confidences about their depression private, there are important limits you need to maintain. If anyone ever shares that they're thinking of suicide or that they wish they would die, or hints in other ways that they may hurt themselves or someone else, you must share that information with or without their permission. Tell a responsible adult immediately.

It's good to know that depressive illness is treatable. With help, you (or your friend) can get better. Most teenagers who receive treatment improve and many never experience another depression.

Maintaining your sources of support. Your circle of support is key to avoiding or recovering from depression. When you think about the people you are close to, consider how much you confide and how much you keep private. It's okay to want your privacy, but the experience of talking with people, adults or other teens, may give you a chance to clarify your own thoughts and get some helpful new insights. Similarly, consider your responses to others. Do you jump in with suggestions or are you able to listen empathically— to express your compassion and understanding of what others are going through?

Problems in your relationships can cause depression—but depression can also cause problems in your relationships. It pays to think about the people in your life and put some effort into keeping these relationships healthy and strong. This can mean reaching out to make new friends as well as being sure to attend to and nurture established friendships. And sometimes managing relationships can mean knowing how and when to let them go. By taking the time and energy to develop strong friendships and positive relationships with important people in your life, you will build a solid social safety net to provide you with support during challenging times and to cheer you on when times are good.

Journal Idea

Jot down some notes about your relationships with others. Do you need to meet new friends? Pay more attention to current friends? Reconnect to old friends? Do you have friends who will be there for you during tough times? Are you there for them when they need you? What adults in your life could you reach out to when you are having difficulty? Do you need to strengthen those bonds? Make a written plan of ways to improve one or more of your connections to other people.

In a Nutshell

1. Focusing on your relationships is important because the support provided by others can make you more emotionally resilient.

2. You will likely be most effective in making new friends with others who share your interests, so becoming more active in something you like could be a good strategy. Assess whether you are being friendly and seeming available to others.

3. While having a boyfriend or girlfriend can be uplifting, it can also be complicated. Relationships also may bring emotional challenges. If a relationship is fraught with conflict and "emotional drama," it may not be healthy for you.

CHAPTER 11
SUMMING IT UP TO SURVIVE AND THRIVE

Being depressed can make it seem as if you're trapped and helpless in the bottom of a deep well. Depression can close in on you and limit your view of the wider world. It can separate you from people you care about and who care about you. Your thinking and behavior can become distorted. Think of the ideas presented in this book as a rope ladder to climb out of that dark place. No one step will bring you to the surface. When you take those first steps, the way out may seem far away and you may find that the ladder is still pretty shaky. With each movement forward, however, you will be closer and closer to overcoming depression. As you make progress, the light and warmth will encourage you to keep going, making later steps to progress easier.

Remember, you have identified a range of actions that can help you reach the surface:

- Reach out to others
- Recognize strengths
- Care for your body
- Use coping strategies
- Be assertive
- Solve problems

- Challenge thoughts
- Change behavior
- Set goals

Whether you've worked your way through this book systematically or simply looked at parts of it that grabbed your interest, you've discovered many ideas about how to protect yourself from, deal with, and overcome depression. You may have tried some of the strategies to see if they're helpful to you. While it's fine to try these techniques in a hit-or-miss way, you'll likely find them even more effective if you use them to develop a plan for yourself. Most of us use planning to protect and care for ourselves in other ways: You go to the doctor for check-ups and vaccinations, you go to the dentist to care for your teeth, you plan for your education, you make plans for school vacations, and so on. But the importance of being proactive (that is, planful) about emotional well-being is often overlooked. Think of it as plotting out the steps of your escape ladder. If you've been writing in your journal or making notes while doing exercises, you have the beginnings of a plan already. Review what you've noted down and consider what other ideas you want to add to your plan. Be sure to include how you will be aware when signs of depression (be they thoughts, behaviors, or feelings) arise. This can include the signs themselves ("I need to be alert to times when I'm avoiding my friends") or situations you know trigger depression for you ("When I think I've been criticized, I know I turn on myself with destructive self-talk").

When you catch yourself falling into depression, or stuck there, plan to carefully analyze and describe all the thoughts, feelings, and behaviors you are experiencing. Keep in mind that the more self-aware you become, the more opportunities you will give yourself to take the small but meaningful steps required to not only survive depression but to really thrive and grow past it.

Once you've identified your depressive thoughts, hold them up to the light of reason and challenge them. How is your thinking distorted and inaccurate? What more realistic thoughts can you grab hold of to pull yourself up?

Consider how you can change depressed behaviors in small or larger ways. Are there problems you can effectively address? Is your behavior pulling you down further? Are you withdrawing from those who might offer support or avoiding challenges you might, with effort, be able to manage? What coping strategies can you employ that have worked for you in the past? What new ones might be worth trying?

FOUR A'S OF COMBATING DEPRESSION: ANTICIPATE, ARTICULATE, ARGUE, ACTION

Anticipate—Don't merely wait for the next time depression hits. Be proactive by making a plan now to recognize the ways in which the depressive process starts, and nip it in the bud.

Articulate—Identify the thoughts, feelings, and behaviors you are experiencing that may be signs you are falling into depression.

Argue—Challenge depressive thoughts and replace them with healthier, more realistic thoughts.

Action—Develop your strengths and work to strengthen your support system. Make changes in your behavior to replace depressive habits with problem solving and active coping.

While you're working on overcoming depression, remember that to reduce the time and energy you devote to attending to it, you need to fill that mind space with more positive things. Don't focus simply on depression or dealing with problems in your life. Remember that to really overcome depression and truly thrive, you'll have to keep your eye on the good things in your life. Celebrate small victories, not just major life successes. Be happy for pleasant time with family and friends or even by yourself. Shine your spotlight on the good things in your life that happen so commonly that you may be overlooking them. Let yourself be proud and confident because of your own special talents, competencies, and strengths.

Journal Idea

Look through your prior journal entries as well as any notes you took while doing exercises. Think about which ones are most helpful to you when you're depressed. Which will help you avoid having the type of experiences that start you on a downward spiral? Which will contribute to building your resiliency? Make a plan to improve your mental resiliency and to cue yourself in ways to combat depression in the future.

APPENDIX

DEPRESSIVE DIAGNOSES

The *Diagnostic and Statistical Manual of Mental Disorders, Fifth Edition* describes a number of depressive disorders. The ones typically seen in teens are:

Adjustment Disorder With Depressed Mood. Several adjustment disorders can occur in response to an identifiable stress, one of which is *adjustment disorder with depressed mood.* It is not uncommon to experience a strong reaction to such stresses as the breakup of a relationship, a natural disaster, a difficult illness, and so forth. But your reaction is expected to be in proportion to the stress, not cause interference to your social and academic functioning, and subside within six months of the stress. If your mood is low and you are teary and have a sense of hopelessness within three months of the stress, or if your distress is out of proportion and interfering with your life in notable ways and fails to subside within six months, then you might have an adjustment disorder. This is certainly the most common depressive diagnosis.

Persistent Depressive Disorder (Dysthymia). *Persistent depressive disorder* is characterized by a depressed or highly irritable mood that is present most of the time over the course of a full year, with no more than a two month symptom-free period. If you are chronically sad or grumpy, you may have gotten so used to it that you don't recognize your mood as a problem. Teens with this disorder may be drawn to alcohol, tobacco, or illegal substances in a misguided attempt to try to block or dampen their emotions. In fact, this may be why you are seeing a doctor. Once you receive the proper diagnosis, you will learn safer and more reliable ways to manage your mood.

Premenstrual Dysphoric Disorder. Obviously, *premenstrual dysphoric disorder* occurs only in females. While it is nearly universal to experience mild premenstrual changes, girls with *premenstrual dysphoric disorder* have moodiness, irritability, anxiety, and uneasiness in addition to several behavioral and physical symptoms, all of which go away only to return the next month, and which have a significant impact on academic work or social functioning. This disorder occurs in less than 2 percent of women. Your doctor will want you to keep a symptom record for at least two months before making this diagnosis.

Major Depressive Disorder. *Major depressive disorder* is relatively common after puberty and most prevalent in the teenage years. If you have developed a depressed or irritable mood or loss of interest or pleasure most of the day, nearly every day, and it has lasted at least two weeks, this diagnosis will be considered. Fatigue and sleep disturbance are often present as well. Since some people experience a *major depressive disorder* and then recover spontaneously, your doctor will want to hear about your past experiences with similar symptoms. Whether this is your first experience with depression or you've had a previous episode, most people improve with treatment.

There are rare cases of depression in response to medication or other substances and depression in response to a medical condition that your doctor can discuss with you. One more class of disorders deserves mention: *bipolar and related disorders*. These are classified separately from the spectrum of depressive disorders, and are distinguished by the presence of mania.

BIPOLAR AND RELATED DIAGNOSES

The *bipolar disorders* are relatively rare despite how frequently you hear people toss around the term. A key feature of the bipolar disorders (and there are several varieties) is manic behavior. Mania is characterized by abnormally and persistently elevated, expansive, or irritable mood. People who are experiencing this mood change may have increased activity, decreased sleep, reckless or foolish behavior, inflated self-appraisal, loud, rapid speech, and/or racing thoughts. These changes in behavior are not your everyday teenage exuberance, they really stand out, and they seriously interfere with life. Mania can alternate with depression or stand alone, and mood shifts can be very rapid. It is essential that people with *bipolar disorders* receive treatment, which is typically provided by a team of specialists, including a psychiatrist who will prescribe medication.

RESOURCES

CHAPTER 1

Allen, N. B. & Sheeber, L. B. (Eds.) (2009). *Adolescent emotional development and the emergence of depressive disorders*. New York: Cambridge University Press.

American Psychiatric Association. (2013). *Diagnostic and statistical manual of mental disorders (Fifth ed.)* Arlington, VA: American Psychiatric Publishing.

American Psychological Association. (n.d.). Teen suicide is preventable. Retrieved from http://www.apa.org/research/action/suicide.aspx

Klein, D. N., Doughtery, L. R., Laptook, R. S., & Olino, T. M. (2009). Temperament and risk for mood disorders in adolescents. In Nicholas B. Allen & Lisa Sheeber (Eds.), *Adolescent emotional development and the emergence of depressive disorders*. Cambridge, United Kingdom: Cambridge University Press.

Lamia, M. (2013). *Emotions! Making sense of your feelings*. Washington, D.C.: Magination Press.

The National Institutes of Health. (n.d.). The teen brain: Still under construction. Retrieved from http://www.nimh.nih.gov/health/publications/the-teen-brain-still-under-construction/index.shtml

Wells, A. (2009). *Metacognitive therapy for anxiety and depression*. New York: Guilford Press.

Whelan, Y. M., Leibenluft, E., Stringaris, A., & Barker, E. D. (2015). From maternal depressive symptoms to adolescent depressive symptoms: The unique contribution of irritability symptoms. *Journal of Child Psychology and Psychiatry*, 56(10), 1092–1100. doi:10.1111/jcpp.12395

CHAPTER 3

Klein, J. S., Jacobs, R. H., & Reinecke, M. A. (2007). Cognitive behavioral therapy for adolescent depression: A meta-analytic investigation of changes in effect-size estimates. *Journal of the American Academy of Child and Adolescent Psychiatry*, 46(11), 1403–1413.

Lamia, M. (2013). *Emotions! Making sense of your feelings*. Washington, D.C.: Magination Press.

CHAPTER 4

Burns, D. D. (2000). *Feeling good: The new mood therapy* (Reprint ed.). New York: HarperCollins.

Covey, S. (2014). *The 7 habits of highly effective teens*. New York: Touchstone/ Simon & Schuster.

Lejues, C. W, Hopko, D. R., & Hopko, S.D. (2001). A brief behavioral activation treatment for depression: Treatment manual. *Behavior Modification 25*(2), 255–286.

Martell, C. R., Addis, M. E., & Jacobson, N. S. (2001). *Depression in context: Strategies for guided action*. New York: W.W. Norton.

CHAPTER 5

Burns, D. D. (1980). *Feeling good: The new mood therapy*. New York: HarperCollins.

Wells, A. (2009). *Metacognitive therapy for anxiety and depression*. New York: Guilford Press.

Winch, G. (2013). *Emotional first aid: Practical strategies for treating failure, rejection, guilt, and other everyday psychological injuries*. New York: Hudson Street Press.

CHAPTER 7

Fristad, M. A., Arnold, J. S. G, & Leffler, J. M. (2011). *Psychotherapy for children with bipolar and depressive disorders*. New York: Guilford Press.

CHAPTER 8

Dunn, A. L., & Weintraub, P. (2008). Exercise in the prevention and treatment of adolescent depression: A promising but little researched intervention. *American Journal of Lifestyle Medicine, 2*(6), 507–518.

Jacka, F. N., Kremer, P. J., Leslie, E. R., Berk, M., Patton, G. C., Toumbourou, J. W., & Williams, J. W. (2010). Associations between diet quality and depressed mood in adolescents: Results from the Australian healthy neighbourhoods study. *Australian & New Zealand Journal of Psychiatry, 44*(5), 435–442.

Jorm, A. F., Morgan, A. J., & Hetrick, S. E. (2008). Relaxation for depression. *Cochrane Database of Systematic Reviews, 4*, Article No: CD007142.

Su, K. P., Lai, H. C., Yang, H. T., Su, W. P., Peng, C. Y., Chang, J. P. C., Chang, H. C., & Pariante, C. M. (2014). Omega-3 fatty acids in the prevention of interferon-alpha-induced depression: Results from a randomized, controlled trial. *Biological Psychiatry, 76*(7), 559–566. doi:10.1016/j.biopsych.2014.01.008

CHAPTER 9

Seligman, M. E. P. (2011). *Flourish: A visionary new understanding of happiness and well-being.* New York: Free Press.

CHAPTER 10

Martin-Storey, A., & Crosnoe, R. (2012). Sexual minority status, peer harassment, and adolescent depression. *Journal of Adolescence, 35*(4), 1001–1011.

Mufson, L., Dorta, K. P., Moreau, D., & Weissman, M. M. (2004). *Interpersonal psychotherapy for depressed adolescents.* New York: Guilford Press.

INDEX

ABOUT THE AUTHORS

Jacqueline B. Toner, PhD, is the co-author of several self-help books. She has been in private practice working with children, teens, and families for over thirty years. Dr. Toner earned her PhD from the University of Virginia and completed two post-doctoral programs (in pediatric psychology and adolescent medicine) at the University of Maryland Medical School. Dr. Toner also serves as lead facilitator and consultant on a project on medical ethics led by Johns Hopkins Hospital and the University of Pittsburgh Medical Center. She is the mother of three grown children and lives with her husband in Baltimore.

Claire A. B. Freeland, PhD, is a clinical psychologist in private practice, working for more than thirty-five years with youth and their families. Interested in bringing the general principles of cognitive-behavioral therapy to families everywhere, she is the co-author, with Dr. Jacqueline Toner, of *What to Do When It's Not Fair*, *What to Do When Mistakes Make You Quake*, and *What to Do When You Feel Too Shy*. She lives with her husband in Baltimore. They have two grown children.

ABOUT MAGINATION PRESS

Magination Press is an imprint of the American Psychological Association, the largest scientific and professional organization representing psychologists in the United States and the largest association of psychologists worldwide.